RANCH HOUSE BAKING MIX

In memory of our mom

Bertha D. Reese

and Grandmother

Amelia Toroni.

Thank you for your love, dedication,

Excellent Cooking

and service to the nation.

Chris & Diana Reese

Bertha D. Reese

A passion for cooking

passed from generation to generation.

Amelia Toroni

The
Ranch House Baking Mix
Cookbook
By
Bertha D. Reese

VOLUME 2

CONTENTS

Recipes from 1 to 322:   Volume 1
Recipes from 323 to 598:   Volume 2
Bonus Recipes: Volumes 1 and 2

1977 - 1982

INTRODUCTION

Ranch House Baking mix is an all-purpose mix that will assist you in making biscuits, waffles, light tender crepes, cakes and many other foods that taste homemade. You can quickly make big ranch-style biscuits, tender muffins and rich short-cakes just like the ones country cooks serve to hungry ranch crews, families and friends.

The seed to formulate a baking mix germinated during a busy period in my life. Pressed for time, I had resorted to using commercial baking mixes and store-bought biscuits and shortcakes, which didn't escape the attention of my family. They were used to being served the big golden-crusted biscuits and rich shortcakes my mother taught me to make when I was a young girl growing up in the country, many years ago.

When I left the country for city life as a young adult, to pursue a career in San Francisco, a copy of the family cookbook containing all my favorite recipes was tucked into my luggage before I left. Through the years the well-used recipe book remained a faithful companion to me.

When I bake a pan of fragrant orange-Frost Gingerbread, or big Ginger Cookies it still evokes memories of cool autumn days in the country, hiking with my brothers and sisters when I was a young girl, on the sylvan forest trails that bordered my father's property. Brightly colored leaves crackled underfoot as we walked about, munching rosy-cheeked autumn apples and spicy cookies. My Ranch House Baking Mix Cookbook contains many recipes based on the favorites served during my childhood years.

We all like compliments for our cooking: when praised after serving a new taste-pleasing dish, we glow with pride then try to surprise the family again with another new treat. Feeling a little guilty over serving packaged biscuits and shortcakes, which were not well received by the family, I started to experiment with formulating a baking mix. After a multitude of trials and errors I finally produced one that received high praise from the family. The more I used the baking mix that I had originally formulated just for biscuits, pancakes, waffles and shortcakes, the more versatile it proved to be. In time my burgeoning baking mix recipe file blossomed into a thick volume bulging with over 380 recipes.

This baking mix cookbook is an

answer to the busy homemaker and career woman/homemakers oft-voiced complaint, "I wish I had more time for home-baking". Not to overlook the bachelor and bachelorettes, they too can benefit from using this cookbook. You can enjoy eating big ranch-style biscuits or dainty little tea biscuits, coffee cakes, cookies and many other treats that taste just like homemade. An added bonus, a homemade baking mix costs much less to make than purchasing supermarket mixes.

BAKING MIX FORMULA INFORMATION

Before mixing the formula, assemble all the ingredients listed. Assemble the utensils needed for measuring and mixing the formula; bowl, measuring cups and spoons, pastry blender, etc. Select a mixing bowl large enough to allow room to thoroughly blend the ingredients together without spillage. The volume of flour should be approximately 1/2 the depth of the mixing bowl. If the container is not large enough, the pastry blender will be too deeply immersed in the flour to satisfactorily blend the ingredients together. Any suitable metal, plastic or glazed pottery mixing bowl can be used. A large cooking pot can also be used if a suitable mixing bowl isn't available. If you possess an extra-large professional cook's mixing bowl, a double batch of the formula can be mixed in the bowl.

Select a good quality all-purpose enriched flour, bleached and pre-sifted at the factory. A name-brand flour will give the best baking results. This also applies to the solid shortening selection.

When time permits make ahead as many batches of the baking mix as you wish. Stored in a cool dry place, it will remain usable up to 6 months.

STORAGE CONTAINERS: The best containers are empty 3-pound solid shortening cans. The wide opening conveniently allows spooning the baking mix into a measuring cup. To prepare for storage, heat the empty can in a warm oven until the residual shortening melts. Pour into a small jar or custard cup for future use. Wipe inside of can dry with paper towels. No need to wash the can before filling with baking mix.

Each can holds approximately 7 cups of the mix. Cover can with the plastic lid to ensure locking out moisture. Until you accumulate enough empty shortening cans for storage, metal flour or sugar canisters can be used. Empty quart-size fruit or mayonnaise jars can also be utilized for storage.

TIME-SAVING TIPS: Batches of baking mix can be quickly prepared by employing this time-saving device. It will also preclude a disappointing discovery when you are ready to prepare a batch of the mix; not having an essential ingredient on hand. The baking powder, sugar, salt, cornstarch, cream of tartar and baking soda can be pre-measured for each batch of the formula. Stir the ingredients together in a 1-cup measure, then store in empty baking powder cans or small glass jars. Close tightly; label tops of containers. Store in a cool dry place until needed.

Another time-saver is to pre-select recipes before making a batch of baking mix. Measure out the amount of prepared baking mix needed for each recipe. Place in plastic storage containers or glass jars. Cover tightly. Place labels or strips of freezer tape on container lids. With a marking pen note name of the recipe to be used, and the amount of baking mix in the container.

RANCH HOUSE BAKING MIX FORMULA

8 cups all-purpose flour
1/4 cup double-acting baking powder
3 tablespoons sugar
1 tablespoon non-iodized salt
1 tablespoon cornstarch
2 teaspoons cream of tartar
1 teaspoon baking soda
1 1/2 cups solid vegetable shortening

    without aerating flour scoop directly from sack or container into a 4 or 8-cup measure. Place flour into a large metal, plastic or glazed pottery mixing bowl; set aside.

    Combine baking powder, sugar, salt, cornstarch, cream of tartar and baking soda in a 1-cup measure. Stir with a fork until well mixed; sprinkle over flour. Stir with a pastry blender until mixture is well blended. Do not under mix as flour is being aerated at this point. Distribute shortening over surface of flour by dropping spoonfuls. Cut in with pastry blender until fine particles begin to form. Scrape pastry blender occasionally with a knife, letting the shortening adhering to the tines of the blender drop back into the flour mixture. Continue mixing until the baking mix particles start clinging together slightly. Transfer to storage containers. Cover tightly and store in a cool dry place up to 6 months. Makes approximately 11 1/2 cups baking mix.

RECIPE PREPARATION

Follow the steps listed below before you start to make a dish. Be accurate in measuring the baking mix and liquid to ensure successful results.

1- Read through the recipe until you thoroughly understand the directions.

2- Assemble all the utensils needed to prepare the recipe; mixing bowl, measuring cups and spoons, beaters, pans, etc. Use nesting-type measuring cups for the baking mix. This will allow you to level off the baking mix with accuracy. Use a glass measuring cup for the liquids to give the most accurate measure. Prepare the baking pans as directed.

3- Assemble all the ingredients listed in recipe. If eggs are listed, use large size.

4- Preheat oven, allowing 15 to 20 minutes before commencing baking. Individual oven temperatures can vary greatly if not calibrated or insulated properly. Increase or decrease oven temperature if necessary, in order to bake the dish in the time specified in recipe. (always allow enough time to preheat oven, whether for baking or reheating food.)

5- MEASURING BAKING MIX: Lightly spoon baking mix into metal or plastic nesting-type measuring cup until fully rounded above top. Level off with flat side of knife or thin metal spatula; avoid packing down. TIP: To catch spills, place measuring cup in a small shallow bowl before spooning in baking mix. after leveling off, pour excess back into baking mix container.

6 - MEASURING LIQUID: Place glass measuring cup on a level surface. Fill to level indicated in recipe. Read at eye level to obtain an accurate measure.

7 - TIMING: If you don't have a kitchen timer, use the sweep second hand on the kitchen clock or your wrist watch to time mixing periods. Start timing as beating commences. Stop and scrape bowl when indicated. Resume timing after scraping is completed.

8 - CORRECTIONS: If an error has been made while measuring the baking mix or liquid, or if the baking mix has settled in the container, additional liquid or baking mix may be required. The corrections can be done just before the the mixing is completed.

If the batter or dough seems too stiff, beat in a small amount of liquid for batter, and stir in for dough, just until blended.

If batter or dough seems too thin, add a small amount of baking mix. Quickly beat in for batter, and stir in for dough, just until blended.

If eggs are included in recipe, use the large size, not extra large or jumbo eggs. If using eggs smaller than the recommended size, a slight increase in the amount of liquid specified in the recipe may be required.

For many people the highlight of a meal is having dessert. Cookbooks have been devoted entirely to desserts, and there still is volumes that can be written about this international delight. Every country has its favorite dessert, touted as the best in the world. America has a love affair with Apple Pie, and the "chocaholics" swoon over a rich, moist chocolate cake covered with creamy, chocolate fudge frosting.

While making a two-crust apple pie is beyond the scope of any baking mix, there is an enticing array of desserts to choose from in this section. For apple pie lovers there is a delicious Two-Crust Apple Crisp that will substitute for "moms apple pie". If you have a yen for something chocolate, try the Heavenly Chocolate Dessert. It is a boon for the busy cook who wishes to make dessert ahead. Creamy and rich with chocolate flavor, this dessert is never a disappointment. The tangy, crustless Baked Lemon Pie is sure to please the lemon fans. If a novice cook wishes to impress guests with her culinary skills, serve Black Forest Dessert. It tastes impressive but requires the minimum of cooking skills to make and assemble.

Making a pie shell presents no rolling out problems to the cook, when making one of the shells listed in this section. PRESS-IN PASTRY requires no tedious rolling out. Just press the dough into place right in the pie plate.

BANANA CREAM PIE

1 baked 9-inch PRESS-IN PASTRY shell (P-579)

FILLING

2 1/2 tsp unflavored gelatine
1/4 cup cold water
1 3/4 cups milk
1 3 3/4-oz pkg vanilla instant pudding and pie filling mix
1 tsp banana extract
1/2 cups mashed bananas
1 peeled banana
1 1/2 cups whipping cream
1/4 cup confectioners' sugar
1 tsp vanilla extract

Place gelatine and cold water into a metal 1-cup measure; let stand 5 minutes. Dissolve over low heat; set aside.

Place milk, pudding mix and banana extract into a deep small bowl. Beat at low speed until mixture starts to thicken. With beaters going at low speed pour in gelatine in a steady stream. Continue beating 1 minute. Remove 1 cup of the filling to a small bowl. Stir in 1/2 cup mashed bananas. Slice the peeled banana into the bottom of cooled pastry shell. Spoon the mashed banana mixture over the banana layer; set aside.

Beat cream in medium bowl just until it begins to hold its shape. Add confectioners' sugar and vanilla. Beat until stiff. Fold 1 1/4 cups of the whipped cream into remaining pudding mix. Spoon over banana mixture in pastry shell. Spread to make an even layer. Chill 3 hours. Spread with remaining whipped cream. Chill 1 hour. Makes 6 to 8 servings.

BAVARIAN CHOCOLATE CREME PIE

325

1 baked 8-inch CHOCOLATE PRESS-IN PASTRY shell (P-577)

FILLING
2 egg yolks
1 tsp vanilla extract
3 tbsp butter
3 tbsp cocoa
2 tbsp sugar
4 tsp hot water
1 1/4 tsp unflavored gelatine
2 tbsp cold water
1 envelope Dessert Topping mix
6 tbsp light cream
1 egg white
1/8 tsp cream of tartar
2 tbsp sugar

WHIPPED CREAM TOPPING
3/4 cup whipping cream
2 tbsp confectioners' sugar
1/2 tsp vanilla extract

FILLING: Beat egg yolks and vanilla together in a small custard cup with a fork; set aside. Melt butter in small saucepan over low heat. Stir in cocoa and sugar. Remove saucepan from heat. Stir in hot water. Beat in egg yolks with a spoon until well mixed; set aside.

Place gelatine and water in a metal 1-cup measure; let stand 5 minutes. Dissolve over low heat. Cool.

Combine topping mix and cream in a deep medium bowl. Beat at low speed 1 minute, then beat at high speed until almost fully whipped. With beaters going at low speed pour in gelatine in a steady stream. Continue whipping at high speed until topping is stiff; set aside. Beat egg white and cream of tartar in small bowl until foamy. Beat in sugar at high speed,

1 tablespoon at a time. Continue beating until stiff but not dry. Gradually fold egg white into chocolate mixture in saucepan. Gradually fold in whipped topping. Pour into cooled pastry shell. Chill 3 hours. Spread with whipped cream topping. Chill 1 hour. Makes 5 to 6 servings.

WHIPPED CREAM TOPPING: Beat cream in small bowl just until it begins to hold its shape. Add confectioners' sugar and vanilla. Beat until stiff.

CHOCOLATE CHEESE REFRIGERATOR PIE

1 baked 9-inch CHOCOLATE PRESS-IN PASTRY shell (P-577)

FILLING
1 8-oz pkg cream cheese
1 1/4 cups milk, divided
2 tbsp sugar
1 4½ oz pkg chocolate instant pudding and pie filling
1 tsp vanilla extract

WHIPPED CREAM TOPPING
3/4 cup whipping cream
2 tbsp confectioners' sugar
3/4 tsp vanilla extract

FILLING: Soften cream cheese in medium bowl. Add 1/4 cup of the milk and 2 tablespoons sugar. Beat until light and creamy, at high speed. Add 3/4 cup more milk and the instant pudding. Beat at medium speed 2 minutes. Scrape bowl. Add remaining milk and vanilla. Beat at low speed 2 minutes. Spoon filling into cooled pastry shell. Chill 5 hours. Spread with whipped cream. Chill 1 hour longer. Makes 6 to 8 servings.

WHIPPED CREAM TOPPING: Beat cream in small bowl just until it begins to hold its shape. Add confectioners' sugar and vanilla. Beat until stiff.

CHOCOLATE MERINGUE PIE

1 baked 9-inch PRESS-IN PASTRY shell (P-579)

FILLING
3 Tbsp butter or margarine
2-oz (2 sqs) unsweetened chocolate
4 egg yolks
½ cup cold milk, divided
¾ cup sugar
¼ cup cornstarch
1½ cups scalded milk
1½ tsp vanilla extract

MERINGUE
1 tbsp cornstarch
2 tbsp cold water
½ cup boiling water
3 egg whites
⅛ tsp cream of tartar
6 Tbsp sugar
1 tsp vanilla extract

FILLING: Melt butter in small saucepan over low heat. Add chocolate; stir until melted. Let saucepan stand on burner with heat off. Place egg yolks and ¼ cup of the cold milk in small bowl. Beat at low speed just until blended. Strain into a 1-cup measure; set aside.

Combine sugar and cornstarch in medium saucepan. Add remaining ¼ cup cold milk; stir until smooth. Gradually pour in scalded milk, stirring constantly. Place saucepan over medium heat. Cook and stir until mixture is thick and smooth. Remove saucepan from heat. Stir in melted chocolate, then gradually stir in egg yolk mixture. Return to low-to-medium heat. Cook and stir until mixture starts to bubble. Reduce heat to low. Continue cooking and stirring until filling thickens. Remove from heat. Stir in vanilla. Cover loosely. Cool 20 minutes, stirring occasionally. Pour filling into cooled pastry shell. Let stand while preparing meringue.

MERINGUE: Combine cornstarch and cold water in small saucepan. Gradually stir in boiling water. Cook and stir over medium heat until clear and thickened. Cover loosely; let stand until cold.

Beat egg whites and cream of tartar in medium bowl until foamy. Gradually beat in sugar, 2 tablespoons at a time. Add vanilla. Continue beating until stiff but not dry. Gradually beat in cold cornstarch mixture, 2 tablespoons at a time, at low speed. Continue beating at high speed 1 minute. Spread meringue over filling to edge of crust.

Bake at 350° 12 minutes or until meringue is lightly browned. Cool on rack 3 hours. Chill 1 to 2 hours. Makes 6 to 8 servings.

CHOCOLATE MOUSSE' PIE

1 baked 9-inch CHOCOLATE PRESS-IN PASTRY Shell
(P-577)

CHOCOLATE FILLING

3 tbsp butter
3/4 cup semi-sweet chocolate chips
3 egg yolks
1 tbsp light or dark rum
1/2 tsp vanilla extract
3 egg whites
1/8 tsp cream of tartar
1/4 cup granulated sugar
1 cup whipping cream
3 tbsp confectioners' sugar
1 tsp vanilla

Melt butter and chocolate chips in double boiler top over hot, not boiling water, with 1/4-inch free space between double boiler top and water. Beat in 1 of the egg yolks, rum and vanilla, at low speed 1/2 minute. Add remaining egg yolks. Beat at medium speed until smooth and well blended. Remove double boiler top from hot water. Cover and set aside while preparing egg whites and whipped cream.

Beat egg whites and cream of tartar in large bowl until foamy. Gradually beat in 1/4 cup sugar, 1 tablespoon at a time. Continue beating until stiff but not dry peaks form; set aside.

With uncleaned beaters beat cream in medium bowl until it just begins to hold its shape. Add confectioners' sugar and vanilla. Beat until stiff; set aside.

Fold 1/4 of the beaten egg whites into the cooled chocolate mixture, then fold the egg white-chocolate mixture into the remaining egg whites. Fold in 1 cup of the whipped cream. (Reserve remaining whipped cream to garnish top.) Spoon filling into cooled pastry shell. Chill 4 hours. Spread reserved whipped cream around the edge of the filling, forming a band 2-inches wide. (Decorate with shaved chocolate if desired.) Chill 1 hour longer. Makes 6 to 8 servings.

COCONUT MERINGUE PIE

1 baked 9-inch BUTTER PRESS-IN PASTRY shell (P-575)

FILLING
4 egg yolks
1/4 cup cold milk
1/2 cup sugar
1/4 cup cornstarch
1/4 cup cold milk
1 1/2 cups scalded milk
3 tbsp butter or margarine
2 tsp vanilla extract
1/2 cup flaked coconut

MERINGUE
1 tbsp cornstarch
2 tbsp cold water
1/2 cup boiling water
3 egg whites
1/8 tsp cream of tartar
6 tbsp sugar
1 tsp vanilla extract
1/2 cup flaked coconut

FILLING: Place egg yolks and 1/4 cup cold milk in small bowl. Beat at low speed just until combined. Strain into a 1-cup measure; set aside.

Combine sugar and cornstarch in medium saucepan. Add 1/4 cup cold milk, stir until smooth. Gradually pour in scalded milk, stirring constantly. Add butter. Place saucepan over medium heat. Cook and stir until mixture is thick and smooth. Remove from heat.

Gradually stir in egg yolk mixture, stirring constantly. Return to low-to-medium heat. Cook and stir until mixture starts to bubble. Reduce heat to low. Continue cooking for a few minutes until filling thickens. Remove from heat. Stir in vanilla. Cover loosely. Cool 20 minutes, stirring occasionally. Sprinkle 1/2 cup coconut in bottom of cooled pastry shell, then pour in filling. Let stand while preparing meringue.

MERINGUE: Combine cornstarch and cold water in small saucepan. Gradually stir in boiling water. Cook and stir over medium heat until clear and thickened. Loosely cover and let stand until cold.

Beat egg whites and cream of tartar in medium bowl until foamy. Gradually beat in sugar, 2 tablespoons at a time. Add vanilla. Continue beating until stiff but not dry. Gradually beat in cold cornstarch mixture, 2 tablespoons at a time, at low speed. Continue beating 1 minute at high speed. Spoon meringue over filling to edge of crust. Sprinkle evenly with 1/2 cup coconut.

Bake at 350° 12 minutes or until meringue is lightly browned. Cool on rack 3 hours. Chill 1 to 2 hours. Makes 6 to 8 servings.

CRUSTLESS BAKED LEMON PIE

FILLING
1/2 cup butter, softened
1 cup sugar
4 eggs
1/2 cup Ranch House Baking Mix
rind of 1 lemon
6 tbsp lemon juice
1/4 cup water

WHIPPED CREAM TOPPING
3/4 cup whipping cream
2 tbsp confectioners' sugar
3/4 tsp vanilla extract

FILLING: Combine butter, sugar and 1 of the eggs in medium bowl. Beat at high speed until light and fluffy. Add remaining eggs, one at a time, beating well after each addition. Add baking mix, beat at medium speed 2 minutes. Scrape bowl with a rubber spatula. Grate lemon rind over mixture. Add lemon juice and water. Beat at low speed 1/2 minute. Scrape bowl. Coat a 9-inch glass pie pan with non-stick vegetable spray. Let stand 5 minutes, then grease pan with vegetable shortening. Pour in filling.

Bake at 350° 25 minutes or until a tester inserted at center comes out slightly moist. Cool pie on rack 1 hour, then chill 4 hours. Spread with topping. Makes 6 to 8 servings.

WHIPPED CREAM TOPPING: Beat cream in small bowl just until it begins to hold its shape. Add confectioners' sugar and vanilla. Beat until stiff.

DEEP DISH APPLE PIE

PASTRY

1 1/4 cups Ranch House Baking Mix
1/4 tsp sugar
2 1/2 tbsp Vegetable shortening
2 to 2 1/2 tbsp cold water

FILLING

8 cups peeled thinly sliced apples
3/4 cup granulated sugar
1/4 cup brown sugar, pkd
2 tbsp cornstarch
1/2 tsp cinnamon
1/8 tsp each nutmeg and salt
1/4 cup butter or margarine, cut into small pieces

PREPARE PASTRY: Place baking mix and sugar into small bowl. Cut in shortening with a pastry blender until coarse particles form. Gradually sprinkle cold water over mixture, blending together with a fork; add just enough water to form a pliable dough. Round up into a smooth ball. Line a 9-inch square baking pan with foil. Lightly dust bottom with flour. Place tablespoons of dough at close intervals on bottom of pan. Press with fingers to make an even layer. Chill while preparing apples.

FILLING: Place apples into large bowl. Combine granulated and brown sugar, cornstarch, spices and salt in small bowl. Stir into apples. Spoon into a lightly buttered 8-inch square glass baking dish. Dot with butter. Cover top of dish with foil, leaving enough overhang to mold snugly around sides. Cut 3 vents in foil to allow steam to escape. (Apples will level during baking.) Place dish on a baking sheet.

Bake at 400° 25 minutes. Lower heat to 375°. Immediately remove baking sheet with dish to a cooling rack; remove foil. Remove chilled pastry from refrigerator. Lift foil liner with pastry out of pan. Turn down edges of foil. Carefully ease pastry off foil then place over apples. Let stand 1 minute to soften slightly, then tuck pastry around inside edges of dish. Crimp against sides to anchor. Cut 4 vents in top of pastry. Return baking sheet with pie to oven. Continue baking until apples are tender, about 20 to 25 minutes. If crust starts overbrowning, loosely cover with vented foil. Serve warm with vanilla ice cream. Makes 6 servings.

DEEP DISH PEACH PIE

7 cups peeled sliced peaches
1 cup granulated sugar
1/4 cup brown sugar, pkd
2 tbsp cornstarch
2 tbsp butter or margarine, cut into small pieces
1 recipe PRESS-IN PASTRY TOPPING (P-582)

Place peaches into large bowl. Combine granulated sugar, brown sugar and cornstarch in small bowl. Stir into peaches. Spoon mixture into a lightly buttered 8-inch square baking dish. Dot with butter. Cover top of dish with foil, leaving enough overhang to mold snugly around sides. Cut 3 vents in top of foil to allow steam to escape. (Peaches will level during baking.) Place dish on a baking sheet.

Bake at 375° 45 minutes or until peaches are tender. Cool until lukewarm. Spoon into serving dishes. Top with baked pastry. Makes 6 servings.

PREPARE PASTRY; press into an 8-inch square on a baking sheet. Cut into 6 rectangles with a sharp knife; don't separate pastry.

Bake at 400° 6 to 8 minutes or until a light golden color. Do not overbake. Recut pastry. Cool 5 minutes. Lift onto peaches with a pancake turner.

DELUXE COCONUT CREAM PIE

1 baked 9-inch PRESS-IN PASTRY shell (P-579)

FILLING
1 cup milk
1 cup flaked coconut, pakd in cup
1 envelope unflavored gelatine
1/4 cup water
2 egg yolks
1 tbsp cornstarch
2 egg whites
1/8 tsp each cream of tartar and salt
6 Tbsp sugar
1 3/4 cups whipping cream
1/4 cup confectioners' sugar
1 tsp vanilla extract

Heat milk to scalding in small saucepan. Stir in coconut. Remove from heat.
Cover and let stand 1 hour. Place coconut in a
large strainer over a bowl to catch liquid.
Press coconut firmly with the back of a
tablespoon to extract all the liquid. Let
stand 30 minutes. Reserve milk.

Place gelatine into small saucepan.
Add water; let stand 5 minutes. Dissolve
over low heat. Let stand on burner
with heat off.

Place egg yolks, 1/4 cup of the coconut
milk and cornstarch in small bowl. Beat
at low speed just until combined. Strain
into a 1-cup measure; set aside.

Add remaining coconut milk to gelatine in saucepan. Bring to simmering over medium heat. Stir in the egg yolk mixture. Cook and stir over low heat until thickened and smooth. Remove from heat. Cover, let stand until cold.

Beat egg whites, cream of tartar and salt in medium bowl until foamy. Gradually beat in 6 tablespoons sugar, 2 tablespoons at a time. Beat until stiff but not dry; set aside. With uncleaned beaters beat cream in medium bowl until it just begins to hold its shape. Add 1/4 cup confectioners' sugar and 2 tsp vanilla extract. Beat until stiff; set aside. Gradually fold cold coconut filling into beaten egg whites. Fold in 2 cups of the whipped cream. Sprinkle 1/2 of the drained coconut into the bottom of the cooled pastry shell. Spoon filling over coconut. Chill pie 2 hours. Spread remaining whipped cream over top. Sprinkle remaining coconut over whipped cream. Chill 2 hours. Makes 6 to 8 servings.

FROZEN CHOCOLATE SUNDAE PIE

1 baked 8-inch RICH CHOCOLATE PRESS-IN PASTRY shell (P-584)

FILLING
1 tbsp butter or margarine
3 tbsp hot water
1-oz (1 sq) semi-sweet chocolate
1/2 cup milk chocolate chips
1 cup Half & Half (commercial cream and milk)
1 tsp vanilla extract
1/2 cup whipping cream

HOT FUDGE SAUCE
3 tbsp butter or margarine
1/2 cup light corn syrup
1/2 cup evaporated milk, divided
3/4 cup semi-sweet chocolate chips
1 tsp vanilla extract

FILLING: melt butter in small saucepan over low heat. Add hot water and 1-oz semi-sweet chocolate. Stir until chocolate melts. Add milk chocolate chips. Continue stirring until mixture is smooth. Remove from heat. Gradually stir in Half & Half. Stir in vanilla. Pour mixture into double boiler top. Fill bottom part of double boiler with 2 inches of ice water and a layer of ice cubes. Beat filling over ice water until chilled, around 10 minutes. Replace ice water as the ice cubes melt.

Beat cream in a small bowl until stiff. Fold in 1/3 of the chocolate

mixture, then fold chocolate – cream
mixture into remaining chocolate mixture
in pan. Spoon filling into cooled pastry
shell. Freeze until barely firm, about 3 to 4 hours.
Cut into serving. Place on serving
plates. Top with Hot Fudge Sauce.
If desired, decorate with canned cream topping,
chopped walnuts and a maraschino cherry. Makes 6
serving.

HOT FUDGE SAUCE : Melt butter in
small saucepan. Add corn syrup. Stir
over medium heat until simmering. Stir
in 1/4 cup of the evaporated milk and
the chocolate chips. Cook and stir over
low heat until chocolate chips are
melted. Add remaining 1/4 cup evaporated
milk and vanilla. Cook and stir 1 minute.
Remove from heat. Cover saucepan; let
cool until sauce is very warm. Makes
about 1 1/2 cups sauce.

NOTE: The pie may be made and
frozen the day before serving. Let frozen
pie stand at room temperature until it
softens slightly, about 20 minutes.

GERMAN CHOCOLATE PIE

1 baked 9-inch CHOCOLATE PRESS-IN PASTRY
shell (page - 577)

FILLING
1 8-oz pkg cream cheese
1 1/2 tsp unflavored gelatine
2 Tbsp cold water
2 egg yolks
2 Tbsp confectioners' sugar
1 tsp vanilla extract
2 Tbsp butter or margarine
1 4-oz pkg German's sweet chocolate
2 egg whites
1/8 tsp each cream of tartar and salt
6 Tbsp sugar
1 1/2 cups whipping cream
1/4 cup confectioners' sugar
1 tsp vanilla extract

Soften cream cheese in medium bowl.
Place gelatine into a metal 1-cup measure.
Add water; let stand 5 minutes. Dissolve
over low heat. Cool. Beat into creamed
cheese with a spoon. Stir in egg yolks, 2 tablespoons
confectioners' sugar and 1 tsp vanilla; set aside.

Melt butter in small saucepan over
low heat. Break up chocolate into chunks.
Add to melted butter. Stir over low heat
until melted. Remove from heat. Cool.

Beat egg whites, cream of tartar
and salt in medium bowl until foamy.

Gradually beat in 6 tablespoons sugar, 2 tablespoons at a time. Beat until stiff but not dry; set aside. With uncleaned beaters beat cream in medium bowl until it just begins to hold its shape. Add 1/4 cup confectioners' sugar and 1 teaspoon vanilla. Beat until stiff; set aside.

With uncleaned beaters beat cooled chocolate into cream cheese mixture at medium speed until well blended. Scrape bowl with a rubber spatula. Beat 1 minute at low speed. Fold in beaten egg whites, 1/3 at a time. Fold in 2 cups of the whipped cream. (Reserve remaining whipped cream to garnish top.) Spoon filling into cooled pastry shell. Chill 4 hours. Spread reserved whipped cream around the edge of filling, forming a band 2-inches wide. (Decorate with shaved chocolate if desired.) Chill 2 hours longer. Makes 6 to 8 servings.

LEMON CHEESE PIE

1 baked 9-inch PRESS-IN PASTRY shell (P-579)

FILLING
1 8-oz pkg. cream cheese, softened
6 tbsp sugar
3/4 cup milk
1 4 1/2-oz pkg Lemon instant pudding and pie filling
1/3 cup lemon juice

WHIPPED CREAM TOPPING
3/4 cup whipping cream
2 tbsp confectioners' sugar
3/4 tsp vanilla extract

FILLING: Place cream cheese and sugar into medium bowl. Beat at high speed until smooth and creamy. Gradually beat in milk at low speed. Scrape bowl with a rubber spatula. Add pudding mix and lemon juice. Beat at medium speed 2 minutes. Scrape bowl. Pour filling into cooled pastry shell. Chill 5 hours. Spread with topping. Chill 1 hour. makes 6 to 8 servings.

WHIPPED CREAM TOPPING: Beat cream in small bowl just until it begins to hold its shape. Add confectioners' sugar and vanilla. Beat until stiff.

LEMON MERINGUE PIE

1 baked 9-inch BUTTER PRESS-IN PASTRY shell (P-575)

FILLING
4 egg yolks
6 tbsp lemon juice
3/4 cup sugar
1/4 cup cornstarch
1/3 cup cold water
1 1/3 cups boiling water
1/4 cup butter or margarine
rind of 1 lemon

MERINGUE
1 tbsp cornstarch
2 tbsp orange juice
1/2 cup boiling water
3 egg whites
1/8 tsp cream of tartar
6 tbsp sugar
1 tsp vanilla extract

FILLING: Place egg yolks and lemon juice in small bowl. Beat at low speed just until combined. Strain into a 1-cup measure; set aside. Combine sugar and cornstarch in medium saucepan. Add cold water, stir until smooth. Gradually pour in boiling water, stirring constantly. Add butter. Place saucepan over medium heat. Cook and stir until mixture is thick and smooth. Remove from heat. Gradually stir in egg yolk mixture. Cook and stir over low-to-medium heat until mixture starts to bubble. Reduce heat to low. Cook and stir until filling thickens. Remove from heat. Grate lemon rind over mixture; stir well. Cover loosely. Cool 20 minutes, stirring occasionally. Pour filling into cooled pastry shell. Let stand while preparing meringue.

MERINGUE: Combine cornstarch and orange juice in small saucepan. Gradually stir in boiling water. Cook and stir over medium heat until clear and thickened. Cover loosely and let stand until cold.

Beat egg whites and cream of tartar in medium bowl until foamy. Gradually beat in sugar, 2 tablespoons at a time. Add vanilla. Continue beating until stiff but not dry. Gradually beat in cold cornstarch mixture, 2 tablespoons at a time, at low speed. Continue beating at high speed 1 minute. Spread meringue over filling to edge of crust.

Bake at 350° 12 minutes or until meringue is lightly browned. Cool on rock 3 hours. Chill 1 to 2 hours. Makes 6 to 8 servings.

LEMON REFRIGERATOR PIE

1 baked 9-inch BUTTER PRESS-IN PASTRY shell (P-575)

FILLING
1 8-oz pkg cream cheese
1 cup sweetened condensed milk
1/3 cup lemon juice
rind of 1 lemon

WHIPPED CREAM TOPPING
3/4 cup whipping cream
2 tbsp confectioners' sugar
3/4 tsp vanilla extract

FILLING: Soften cream cheese in medium bowl. Gradually beat in condensed milk at medium speed. Beat in lemon juice at low speed. Scrape bowl with a rubber spatula. Grate lemon rind over mixture. Stir with a spoon until well blended. Pour filling into cooled pastry shell. Chill 5 hours. Spread with topping. Chill 1 hour. Makes 6 to 8 servings.

WHIPPED CREAM TOPPING: Beat cream in small bowl just until it begins to hold its shape. Add confectioners' sugar and vanilla. Beat until stiff.

MINT CREAM PIE

1 baked 9-inch CHOCOLATE PRESS-IN PASTRY shell (P-577)

FILLING

1 envelope unflavored gelatine
1/4 cup cold water
2 egg yolks
1/4 cup milk
1/3 cup green creme de menthe (liqueur)
1/4 tsp peppermint extract
6 drops green food color
2 egg whites
1/4 tsp cream of tartar
1/8 tsp salt
1/4 cup granulated sugar
1 3/4 cups whipping cream
1/4 cup confectioners' sugar
1 1/2 tsp vanilla extract

Place gelatine and cold water into small saucepan; let stand 5 minutes. Dissolve over low heat. Let saucepan stand on burner with heat off. Beat yolks and milk in small bowl just until combined. Strain into the warm gelatine mixture. Cook and stir over low heat until mixture is hot and small bubbles appear around the edges of pan; do not boil. Remove saucepan from heat. Stir in creme de menthe, peppermint extract and food color. Chill until mixture is consistency of unbeaten egg whites. While mixture is chilling, prepare egg whites and whipped cream.

Beat egg whites, cream of tartar and salt in medium bowl until foamy.

Gradually beat in 1/4 cup sugar, 1
tablespoon at a time. Beat until stiff
but not dry; set aside. With uncleaned
beaters whip cream in medium bowl
just until it begins to hold its shape.
Add confectioners' sugar and vanilla.
Beat until stiff; set aside. Gradually
fold chilled mint mixture into beaten
egg whites. Fold in 2 cups of the
whipped cream. Spoon into cooled
pastry shell. Chill 4 hours. Spread
with remaining whipped cream.
Chill 1 hour. Makes 6 to 8 servings.

REFER TO RECIPE 348 — R.H. BACK) FOR FILLING

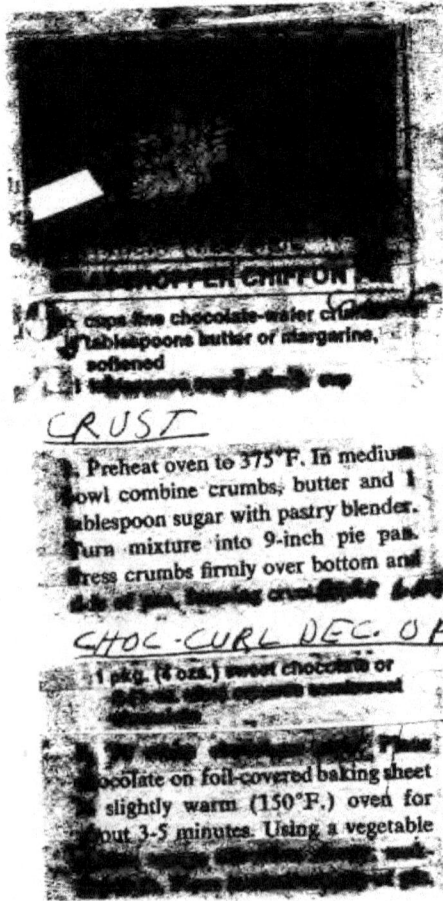

CRUST

Preheat oven to 375°F. In medium
bowl combine crumbs, butter and 1
tablespoon sugar with pastry blender.
Turn mixture into 9-inch pie pan.
Press crumbs firmly over bottom and

CHOC-CURL DEC. OPT

1 pkg. (4 ozs.) sweet chocolate or

chocolate on foil-covered baking sheet
slightly warm (150°F.) oven for
about 3-5 minutes. Using a vegetable

alt- crust
to use with
the mint cream
pie - GOOD RECIPE
Same as
Grasshopper Pie

the filling
may be
adapted for
any flavor
pie by
adjusting
the flavors
as in Recipe
338
adapted for
Deluxe Coconut
Cream Pie

PECAN PIE

1 unbaked 8-inch PRESS-IN PASTRY shell (P-579)

FILLING
6 Tbsp butter or margarine
3/4 cup light corn syrup
2/3 cup brown sugar, pkd
1 1/2 tsp vanilla extract
3 eggs
1 1/4 cups pecan halves

PREPARE SYRUP BASE. Melt butter in medium saucepan. Add syrup and brown sugar. Cook and stir over medium heat until mixture comes to boiling. Remove from heat; stir in vanilla. Cover; cool to lukewarm.

Beat eggs slightly in medium bowl. With beaters going at low speed, pour in cooled syrup in a steady stream. Scrape pan and add residual syrup to egg mixture. Blend at low speed 15 seconds. Stir in pecans. Pour filling into prepared pastry shell. Place pie on a baking sheet.

Bake at 325° 40 to 45 minutes until top is well browned. If pie starts to overbrown, loosely cover top of pie with foil the last 10 to 12 minutes of baking time. Place pie on cooling rack. Let stand until cold, then chill 3 hours. Makes 6 servings.

4 SHELLS
2 tbsp butter or margarine
1/2 cup hot water
1 1/2 tsp sugar
3/4 cup Ranch House Baking mix
2 eggs

6 SHELLS
3 tbsp butter or margarine
3/4 cup hot water
2 tsp sugar
1 cup plus 2 tbsp Ranch House Baking mix
3 eggs

8 SHELLS
1/4 cup butter or margarine
1 cup hot water
1 tbsp sugar
1 1/2 cups Ranch House Baking mix
4 eggs

TO PREPARE 4 SHELLS: Melt butter in small saucepan over low heat. (Use a medium saucepan for 6 to 8 shells.) Add hot water and sugar. Bring to boiling over high heat, then lower heat until water is simmering. Add baking mix. Stir with a wooden spoon until mixture forms a smooth ball, about 1 minute. Turn heat off; continue stirring 1 minute. Remove saucepan from heat; cool 1 minute. Add 1 egg. (Add 2 eggs for 6 to 8 shells.) Beat with a spoon until smooth. Add remaining egg. Beat with electric mixer at medium speed 1 minute. Scrape sides and bottom of pan with a rubber spatula. Beat at medium speed 1 minute. Scrape pan; let stand 10 minutes. Drop dough onto a lightly greased baking sheet in 4 equal portions, spacing about 3 1/2 inches apart. With a dinner knife, smooth dough upward into a rounded mound.

Bake at 400° 15 minutes. Lower temperature to 300°. Bake 30 to 35 minutes longer until shells are deep golden in color. Remove to cooling rack with a pancake turner. Let stand until cool enough to handle, about 5 to 8 minutes. With the tip of a small sharp knife, cut into shell near the top, then cut all around to make a 3-inch removable top. Remove any soft portions of dough remaining inside shell. Cool completely.

TO SERVE: Fill with your choice of filling, using about 1/2 cup for each puff. Replace top. Chill or serve immediately.

NOTE: Shells may be baked in advance, then frozen up to 3 months. When ready to serve, thaw shells. Place on a baking sheet. Heat in oven at 350°, uncovered, 8 to 10 minutes. Cool on rack. Fill as directed above.

6 baked DESSERT PUFF SHELLS (P-351)
BAVARIAN CREAM FILLING
1 1/2 tsp unflavored gelatine
2 Tbsp cold water
2 egg yolks
3 Tbsp evaporated milk
3 Tbsp flour
3/4 cup scalded milk
1 tsp vanilla extract
2 egg whites
1/8 tsp cream of tartar
1/4 cup sugar
1 recipe CHOCOLATE GLAZE (P-360)

FILLING: Place gelatine and cold water
into a metal 1-cup measure; let stand 5
minutes. Dissolve over low heat. Cool.

Beat egg yolks and evaporated milk
in small deep bowl at medium speed
until creamy. Blend in flour. With beaters
going at low speed, gradually pour in
hot milk. Scrape sides and bottom of
bowl with a rubber spatula. Beat at
low speed 1/2 minute. Transfer mixture
to a small saucepan. Stir in gelatine.
Cook and stir with a wooden spoon
over low heat until filling is thick

and smooth. Spoon into a small bowl.
Stir in vanilla. Cover bowl with plastic wrap.
Let stand until cold, about 1 1/2 hours,
stirring occasionally.

Beat egg whites and cream of
tartar in medium bowl until foamy.
Gradually beat in sugar, 1 tablespoon
at a time. Beat until stiff but not
dry. Fold 1/4 of the egg whites into the
cold filling, then gradually fold egg white-
filling mixture back into remaining
whites, 1/4 at a time. Fill each cooled
shell with 1/2 cup filling; replace top.
Spread tops with Chocolate Glaze.
Chill 3 hours. Makes 6 servings.

BERRY CREAM PUFFS

6 baked DESSERT PUFF SHELLS (P-351)

BERRY CREAM FILLING

1 10-oz pkg sweetened frozen raspberries or
  strawberries, thawed
1 1/3 cups whipping cream
confectioners' sugar
canned cream topping

Place thawed berries into a large strainer over a bowl. Drain 30 minutes; reserve juice.

Beat cream in medium bowl until stiff. Fold in berries and 1 to 2 tablespoons of the reserved juice. Add confectioners' sugar to taste. Fill each cooled shell with 1/2 cup filling; replace top. Place on serving plate. Decorate tops with cream topping; drizzle with remaining juice. Makes 6 servings.

CHOCOLATE CREAM PUFFS

5 baked DESSERT PUFF SHELLS (P-351)
CHOCOLATE FILLING
2 egg yolks
1 tsp Vanilla extract
2 tbsp butter or margarine
1 Tbsp sugar
2 1/2 Tbsp cocoa
1 tsp unflavored gelatine
2 tbsp cold water
1 envelope Dessert Topping mix
6 tbsp light cream or canned dairy vegetable blend
1 egg white
1/8 tsp cream of tartar
2 tbsp sugar
1 recipe CHOCOLATE GLAZE (P-360)

CHOCOLATE FILLING: Beat egg yolks and
Vanilla together in a small custard cup
with a fork; set aside. Melt butter in
small saucepan over low heat. Stir in
1 Tablespoon sugar. Remove from heat.
Stir in cocoa until smooth. Beat in
egg yolks with a spoon; set aside.

Place gelatine and water into a metal
1-cup measure; let stand 5 minutes.
Dissolve over low heat. Cool.

Combine topping mix and cream in
a deep medium bowl. Beat at low
speed 1 minute. Increase to high speed,
beat until almost fully whipped. With
beaters going on low speed, pour in
gelatine in a steady stream. Continue

whipping at high speed until topping is stiff; set aside.

Beat egg white and cream of tartar in small bowl until foamy. Beat in sugar, 1 tablespoon at a time at high speed. Beat until stiff but not dry. Gradually fold beaten egg white into chocolate mixture in saucepan. Gradually fold in whipped topping. Chill 15 minutes. Fill each cooled shell with 1/2 cup filling; replace top. Spread glaze over tops. Chill 3 hours. makes 5 servings.

8 baked DESSERT PUFF SHELLS (P-351)
COCONUT CUSTARD FILLING
2 cups milk
3 tbsp butter or margarine
2 tsp vanilla extract
4 egg yolks
1/2 cup sugar
1/4 cup cornstarch
1/2 cup flaked coconut, pkd
1/2 cup whipping cream
1 recipe CHOCOLATE GLAZE (P-360)

FILLING: Place milk, butter and vanilla into medium saucepan. Scald over low heat while preparing egg yolk mixture. (Do not boil.)

Beat egg yolks and sugar in medium bowl at high speed 5 minutes. Add cornstarch. Stir with beaters to dampen, beat at low speed until well blended. With beaters going at low speed, gradually pour in hot milk. Scrape sides and bottom of bowl with a rubber spatula. Beat at low speed 1/2 minute. Rinse saucepan, then pour in milk mixture. Cook and stir with a wooden spoon over low-to-medium heat until filling is thick and smooth. Pour into medium bowl. Beat at medium speed 2 minutes.

Stir in coconut. Cover bowl with plastic wrap. Cool 30 minutes; then transfer to refrigerator. Chill until cold, about 30 to 40 minutes. Beat cream in small bowl until stiff. Beat chilled custard with a spoon until smooth, then gradually fold in whipped cream. Fill each cooled shell with 1/2 cup filling; replace top. Spread tops with Chocolate Glaze. Chill until serving time. Makes 8 servings.

CREAM PUFFS

6 baked DESSERT PUFF SHELLS (Page -351)

WHIPPED CREAM FILLING
1 tsp unflavored gelatine
1 1/2 tbsp cold water
1 1/2 cups whipping cream
1/4 cup confectioners' sugar
1 1/2 tsp vanilla extract

CHOCOLATE GLAZE
1 tbsp butter or margarine
1/2 tbsp hot water
1/2 tbsp light corn syrup
2 tbsp cocoa
3/4 cup confectioners' sugar
1 tbsp evaporated milk
1/2 tsp vanilla extract

WHIPPED CREAM FILLING · Place gelatine and cold water into a metal 1-cup measure; let stand 5 minutes. Dissolve over low heat · Cool.

Beat cream in medium bowl just until it begins to hold its shape · Add confectioners' sugar and vanilla · Beat at low speed 10 seconds · With beaters going at low speed pour in gelatine in a steady stream · Beat until stiff · Fill each cooled shell with 1/2 cup whipped cream; replace top · Spread tops with Chocolate Glaze · Chill 3 hours · makes 6 servings.

2- *near* *cups*

CHOCOLATE GLAZE: melt butter in small saucepan over low heat. Stir in hot water, corn syrup and cocoa. Remove from heat. Cool. Stir in remaining ingredients. Beat with spoon until mixture is smooth. Place saucepan over low heat. Stir until glaze is lukewarm and slightly runny. If glaze starts to thicken, place over low heat. Stir until slightly runny.

FRENCH CHOCOLATE CREAM PUFFS

6 baked DESSERT PUFF SHELLS (P-351)
FRENCH CHOCOLATE FILLING
2 egg yolks
1 tsp vanilla extract
2 1/2 tbsp butter or margarine
1/2 cups (3-oz) semi-sweet chocolate chips
1 tsp unflavored gelatine
2 tbsp cold water
1 1/3 cups whipping cream
1/4 cup confectioners' sugar
1 recipe CHOCOLATE GLAZE (P-360)

FRENCH CHOCOLATE FILLING: Beat egg yolks and vanilla together in a small custard cup with a fork; set aside. Melt butter in small saucepan over low heat. Add chocolate, stir until melted. Remove from heat. Beat in egg yolks with a spoon; set aside.

Place gelatine and water into a metal 1-cup measure; let stand 5 minutes. Dissolve over low heat. Cool.

Whip cream in medium bowl just until it begins to hold its shape. Blend in confectioners' sugar. With beaters going on low speed, pour in gelatine in a steady stream. Continue whipping at high speed until stiff. Fold 1/4 into the chocolate mixture, then gradually fold chocolate-whipped cream mixture into remaining whipped cream. Fill each cooled shell with 1/2 cup filling; replace top. Spread glaze over tops. Chill 3 hours. Makes 6 servings.

APPLE CRISP

TOPPING
1 cup Ranch House Baking mix
1/2 cup granulated sugar
1/2 cup brown sugar, pkd
1/2 tsp cinnamon
1/8 tsp nutmeg
1/4 cup butter, cut into small pieces

FILLING
6 cups peeled thinly sliced apples
1/4 cup granulated sugar
1/4 cup brown sugar, pkd
1/4 tsp cinnamon
1/8 tsp nutmeg
2 tbsp butter, cut into small pieces

TOPPING: Combine baking mix, granulated and brown sugar, cinnamon and nutmeg in medium bowl. Cut in butter with a pastry blender until coarse particles form; set aside.

FILLING: Combine apples, granulated and brown sugar, cinnamon and spices in large bowl. Spoon into a buttered 2-quart round glass baking dish. Dot with butter, spacing evenly. Sprinkle topping over apples. Lightly press down to make an even layer.

Bake at 375° 25 minutes. Cut 6 vents in a piece of foil large enough to cover top of baking dish. Continue baking until apples are tender, around 20 minutes for golden delicious, 30 minutes for firmer apples. Remove foil, place dish on cooling rack. Serve warm with vanilla ice cream or whipped cream. Makes 6 servings.

APPLE TORTE

FILLING

2 tbsp butter or margarine
1/3 cup brown sugar, pkd
1/4 tsp cinnamon
#1/16 tsp nutmeg
2 tbsp water
3 1/2 cups peeled, thinly sliced apples such
  as Golden delicious (about 3 large apples)

BATTER

3 eggs
1 cup Ranch House Baking mix
3 tbsp each honey, sour cream and
  buttermilk
1 tbsp sugar
1 tsp vanilla extract

FILLING: melt butter in a 9-inch
heavy iron skillet over low heat. Add
brown sugar, spices and water. Cook
and stir over medium heat until mixture
is simmering. Add the sliced apples;
stir well. Cover pan and cook 7 minutes.
Remove cover. Gently stir apples, spoon
the brown sugar mixture over them. Continue
cooking, uncovered, until apples are almost
tender, 7 to 12 minutes, (depending upon the
variety apples used) and the liquid is
reduced to a thick syrup. Stir occasionally.
Spoon apples into a large shallow bowl;
cool while preparing batter. Wash
and dry skillet. Grease well and set

- 2 - apple 3 0

aside.

BATTER: Beat egg in medium bowl until frothy. Add baking mix. Beat at medium speed 1 minute. Scrape bowl with a rubber spatula. Add remaining ingredients. Beat at low speed 2 minutes. Scrape bowl. Pour 2/3 cup of the batter into bottom of the skillet.

Bake at 375° 5 minutes. Remove skillet from oven. Carefully spoon apples over crust. Pour remaining batter over apples. Return to oven. Bake at 375° 20 to 22 minutes until top is golden brown. Cool torte in pan until luke- warm. Serve with whipped cream. Makes 6 servings.

BAKED CHOCOLATE PUDDING

2/3 cup sugar
3 tbsp butter or margarine, softened
2 extra large egg yolks
2 Tbsp water
1 tsp vanilla extract
3 tbsp Ranch House Baking mix
1 1/2 tbsp cocoa
1 cup milk
2 extra large egg whites
1/8 tsp cream of tartar
2 tbsp sugar

Beat sugar, butter and egg yolks in small bowl at medium speed until creamy. Blend in water and vanilla at low speed. Add baking mix and cocoa. Beat at medium speed 2 minutes. Scrape bowl with a rubber spatula. Gradually blend in milk at low speed. Scrape bowl; set aside.

Beat egg whites and cream of tartar in small bowl until foamy. Beat in sugar, 1 tablespoon at a time. Beat until soft peaks form. Gradually stir chocolate mixture into egg whites with a rubber spatula. Pour into 6 buttered 6-oz glass custard cups, dividing evenly. Place cups in a 13 by 9-inch baking pan. Pour in boiling water to 1 inch depth.

Bake at 350° 25 minutes or until a tester inserted 1/2-inch from edge of cup comes out slightly moist. Remove cups from hot water. Place pudding on cooling rack. Let stand until cold. Serve with whipped cream. Makes 6 servings.

NOTE: The pudding may be baked a day or two in advance. Store in refrigerator until serving time.

BAKED LEMON PUDDING

1/2 cup sugar
2 tbsp butter or margarine, softened
2 extra large egg yolks
1/4 cup lemon juice
1/3 cup Ranch House Baking mix
1 cup milk
rind of 1 lemon
2 extra large egg whites
1/8 tsp cream of tartar
2 tbsp sugar

Beat sugar, butter and egg yolks in small bowl at medium speed until creamy. Blend in 1 1/2 tablespoons of the lemon juice at low speed. Add baking mix. Beat at medium speed 2 minutes. Scrape bowl with a rubber spatula. Blend in remaining lemon juice at low speed. Scrape bowl. Gradually blend in milk at low speed. Grate lemon rind over mixture. Scrape bowl, stir 10 turns; set aside.

Beat egg whites and cream of tartar in small bowl until foamy. Beat in sugar, 1 tablespoon at a time. Beat until soft peaks form. Gradually stir lemon mixture into egg whites with a rubber spatula. Pour into 6 buttered 6-oz glass custard cups, dividing evenly. Place cups in a 13 by 4-inch baking pan. Pour in boiling water to 1 inch depth.

Bake at 350° 25 minutes or until a tester inserted 1/2-inch from edge of cup comes out slightly moist. Remove cups from hot water. Place pudding on cooling rack. Let stand until cold. Serve with whipped cream. Makes 6 servings.

NOTE: The pudding may be baked a day or two in advance. Store in refrigerator until serving time.

BAKED ORANGE PUDDING

6 tbsp sugar
2 Tbsp butter or margarine, softened
2 extra large egg yolks
1/4 cup frozen orange juice concentrate, thawed
2 tbsp orange flavored instant breakfast drink powder
1/3 cup Ranch House Baking mix
1 cup milk
2 extra large whites
1/8 tsp cream of tartar
2 tbsp sugar

Beat sugar, butter and egg yolks in small bowl at medium speed until creamy. Blend in orange juice concentrate and orange powder at low speed. Add baking mix. Beat at medium speed 2 minutes. Scrape bowl with a rubber spatula. Gradually blend in milk at low speed. Scrape bowl; set aside.

Beat egg whites and cream of tartar in small bowl until foamy. Beat in sugar, 1 tablespoon at a time. Beat until soft peaks form. Gradually stir orange mixture into egg whites with a rubber spatula. Pour into 6 buttered 6-oz glass custard cups, dividing evenly. Place cups in a 13 by 9-inch baking pan. Pour in boiling water to 1 inch depth.

Bake at 350° 25 minutes or until a tester inserted 1/2-inch from edge of cup comes out slightly moist. Remove cups from hot water. Place pudding on cooling rack. Let stand until cold. Serve with whipped cream. Makes 6 servings.

NOTE: The pudding may be baked a day or two in advance. Store in refrigerator.

BLACK FOREST DESSERT

PASTRY
1 cup Ranch House Baking Mix
2 1/2 tbsp sugar
2 tbsp cocoa
2 tbsp butter, softened
1 tbsp beaten egg
1 tbsp cold water

FILLING
9 cups milk
2 4 1/2-oz pkgs chocolate instant pudding and pie filling
1 cup cherry jam

WHIPPED CREAM TOPPING
2 tsp unflavored gelatine
3 tbsp cold water
1 1/2 cups whipping cream
1/4 cup confectioners' sugar
1 1/2 tsp vanilla extract

PASTRY: Combine baking mix, sugar and cocoa in medium bowl. Cut in butter with a pastry blender until coarse particles form. Combine beaten egg and cold water. Sprinkle over cocoa mixture, blending together with a fork until a pliable dough forms. Round up into a smooth ball. Press into a 9-inch square on a lightly greased baking sheet. (If baking sheet has a rim, press dough into upper half of pan, using one of the corner sides of the pan to make shaping easier.) Lightly cut pastry into six 4 1/2 by 3-inch rectangles by cutting in 3rds crosswise, then cutting in half horizontally; don't separate pastry.

Bake at 400° 8 minutes. Immediately recut pastry. Cool in pan 5 minutes, then carefully remove to cooling rack with a pancake turner. Cool.

FILLING: Place milk and chocolate pudding mix into medium bowl. Beat at low speed 3 minutes; set aside.

TOPPING: Place gelatine in a metal 1-cup measure. Add water; let stand 5 minutes. Dissolve gelatine in cup over low heat. Cool.

Beat cream in medium bowl until it just begins to hold its shape. Add confectioners' sugar and vanilla. Beat at low speed 10 seconds. With beaters going at low speed, pour in gelatine in a steady stream. Beat until stiff; set aside.

Spread 2 rounded tablespoons cherry jam over top of each piece of pastry. Carefully spread 1/3 cup chocolate filling over jam. Spoon 1/2 cup whipped cream over chocolate filling. Carefully spread to cover top and sides of dessert. Chill 4 hours. Makes 6 servings.

1 recipe YEAST PASTRY (P-588)
1 30-oz can fruit cocktail, well drained
3/4 cup thick unsweetened applesauce
1/3 cup brown sugar, pkd
1/2 tsp cinnamon

PREPARE YEAST PASTRY; divide into 4 equal portions; set aside.

Combine fruit cocktail, applesauce, brown sugar and cinnamon in small bowl. Butter four 10-oz glass baking dishes. Spoon in fruit mixture, dividing evenly. On a floured surface pat out pastry with floured hand to 4 1/2-inch rounds. Place on top of fruit.

Bake at 350° 30 minutes. Serve warm with Vanilla ice cream. Makes 4 servings.

HEAVENLY CHOCOLATE DESSERT

BATTER
2 tbsp melted butter, cooled
1/2 cup brown sugar, pkd
1/2 cup granulated sugar
1 egg
1 tsp Vanilla extract
1 cup Ranch House Baking mix
6 tbsp cocoa (1/3 cup plus 2 tsp)
1/8 tsp baking soda
3/4 cup water

CHOCOLATE CREAM FILLING
1 envelope unflavored gelatine
1/4 cup cold water
6 tbsp butter
6-oz (6 sqs) semisweet chocolate
6 egg yolks
2 tsp Vanilla extract
3 cups whipping cream
1 1/2 cups confectioners' sugar

BATTER: Beat melted butter, brown and granulated sugar, egg and Vanilla in medium bowl at high speed 8 minutes. Set aside, with beaters positioned over bowl to catch drippings.

In medium bowl stir together baking mix, cocoa and baking soda with a pastry blender until well mixed. Add water. With uncleaned beaters stir to dampen, beat at low speed 1/2 minute. Scrape bowl with a rubber spatula, stir 10 turns. Fold in 1/2 of the egg mixture with a large slotted spoon. Add remaining egg mixture, gently fold in until thoroughly blended. (Batter will be thin.) Pour into greased and floured on bottom 8-inch square baking pan.

Bake at 350° 25 minutes or until center tests done. Cool cake in pan on rack 5 minutes. Loosen edges with a sharp knife; double invert onto cooling rack. Let stand 1 hour, then chill 1 hour.

Foil-line a 10-inch square baking pan, leaving an overhang. Cut chilled cake in half. Tear cake half into 1-inch pieces; layer over bottom of pan. Spoon 1/2 of the filling over cake pieces. With the tip of a tablespoon pat down to flow filling between cake pieces and around edges of pan. Tear apart remaining cake. Repeat with cake pieces and filling. Chill 4 hours. TO SERVE: Cut into 12 portions. Dip a thin bladed knife or metal spatula in hot water. Dry, then run around edges of dessert to loosen. Remove from pan by grasping foil overhang then placing on a flat surface. Turn down foil. Transfer dessert to serving plates with a pancake turner. Makes 12 servings.

CHOCOLATE CREAM FILLING: Place gelatin into a metal 1-cup measure. Add water; let stand 5 minutes. Dissolve gelatin in cup over low heat. Cool.

Melt butter in medium saucepan

over low heat. Add chocolate, stir until melted. Remove from heat. Beat egg yolks and vanilla in small bowl just until blended. Beat 1/2 into chocolate with a spoon. Add remaining egg yolks. Beat until well blended; set aside.

Beat cream in - large bowl until it just begins to hold its shape. Add confectioners' sugar, beat 10 seconds. With beaters going at low speed, pour in gelatine in a steady stream. Continue whipping until stiff. Fold 1/4 of the whipped cream into the chocolate mixture, then gradually fold the chocolate mixture back into the remaining whipped cream.

NOTE: Heavenly Chocolate Dessert may be be made the day before serving. After the filling has set, cover top of pan with plastic wrap.

PEACH COBBLER

FILLING

5 cups peeled sliced peaches
2 tsp lemon juice
1 tsp grated lemon rind
2/3 cup granulated sugar
1/4 cup brown sugar, pkd
2 tbsp cornstarch
2 tbsp butter or margarine, cut into small pieces

TOPPING

1 cup Ranch House Baking mix
1 tbsp sugar
1/2 cup light cream

FILLING: Place peaches into large bowl. Sprinkle with lemon juice. Stir in lemon rind. Combine granulated and brown sugar and cornstarch in small bowl. Stir into peaches. Spoon into a buttered 2-quart round glass baking dish. Dot with butter or margarine.

Bake at 375° 20 minutes, uncovered. Drop tablespoonfuls of topping over peaches. Spread batter with the back of a table-spoon to cover peaches evenly. Continue baking 20 to 25 minutes or until peaches are tender and crust is golden. Place dish on cooling rack. Serve warm with whipped cream. Makes 5 servings.

TOPPING: Combine baking mix and sugar in small bowl. Add cream. Stir with a fork until mixed.

TOPPING
3/4 cup Ranch House Baking Mix
3/4 cup quick-cooking oats
1/2 cup brown sugar, pkd
1/2 tsp cinnamon
1/8 tsp nutmeg
6 tbsp butter, softened

FILLING
2 tbsp butter softened
4 1/2 cups peeld sliced peaches
3 tbsp sugar

TOPPING: Combine baking mix, oats, brown sugar, cinnamon and nutmeg in a medium bowl. Cut in butter with a dinner knife until coarse crumbs form; set aside.

Filling: Spread the 2 tablespoons butter on bottom and 2 inches up the sides of a 1 1/2-quart round glass baking dish. Combine peaches and sugar in large bowl. Spoon into prepared dish. Sprinkle topping evenly over peaches. Lightly press down to make an even layer.

Bake at 375° 15 minutes. Lower oven temperature to 350°. Bake 15 minutes longer or until peaches are tender. If topping starts overbrowning, loosely cover dish with a piece of vented foil. Serve warm. Makes 4 servings.

PEANUT TARTS

4 unbaked TART SHELLS (P-581) made from 1 recipe
   PRESS-IN PASTRY for 10-inch shell (P-579)

FILLING
2 eggs
6 tbsp brown sugar, pkd
1/2 cup light corn syrup
1/4 cup melted butter, cooled
1/2 tsp vanilla extract
1/4 tsp each rum, brandy and coconut extract
3/4 cup medium to finely chopped unsalted peanuts

PREPARE TART SHELLS: Coat four 6-oz
glass baking cups with non-stick vegetable
spray. Press in pastry and shape as directed;
set aside.

FILLING: Beat eggs and brown sugar in
medium bowl at high speed until well blended.
Add syrup, melted butter and extracts. Beat at
low speed just until well mixed. Stir in
chopped peanuts. Pour filling into tart shells,
dividing evenly. Place cups on a baking sheet.

Bake at 350° 28 to 30 minutes until
tarts are well browned. Remove cups from
baking sheet to cooling rack. Let stand
until cold, then chill 2 to 3 hours. Makes
4 servings.

TWO-CRUST APPLE CRISP

BOTTOM CRUST & TOPPING

1 1/4 cups Ranch House Baking mix

2/3 cup brown sugar, pkd

1/2 teaspoon cinnamon

1/8 teaspoon nutmeg

5 tablespoons butter cut into 1/2-inch cubes, then softened slightly

1 cup quick oats

1/2 cup finely chopped walnuts or pecans

FILLING

8 cups peeled, thinly sliced cooking apples, about 8 medium

1/2 cup granulated sugar

1/4 cup brown sugar, pkd

1/3 cup orange juice

1/4 teaspoon cinnamon

1/8 teaspoon nutmeg

1/4 cup cold water

2 Tablespoons cornstarch

BOTTOM CRUST & TOPPING: Combine baking mix, brown sugar and spices in medium bowl. Cut in butter with a pastry blender until a crumbly mixture forms. Stir in oats and chopped nuts with a fork. Lightly grease a 9-inch square baking pan. Spoon 1/2 of the crumb mixture into bottom of pan. Firmly press into place to form an even layer. Set aside remaining crumb mixture for topping. Bake crust at 350° 12 minutes until lightly browned around the edges. Cool.

FILLING: Place apples, granulated sugar, brown sugar, orange juice, cinnamon and nutmeg into a Dutch oven or large saucepan. Bring to boiling over high heat, then stir until well blended. Lower heat until liquid is simmering. Cover. Cook apples until almost tender, about 7 to 10 minutes, depending on the variety of apples; do not overcook. Combine cold water and cornstarch in a 1-cup measure. Carefully stir into simmering apple mixture. Continue cooking and gently stirring as to not break up apples until thickened, about 2 minutes. Remove from heat. Cool to lukewarm, uncovered. Spoon over baked crust. Sprinkle reserved crumb mixture over filling. Lightly press with fingers to make an even layer.

Bake at 350° until apples test tender and crust is golden brown, about 28 to 30 minutes. Serve warm with vanilla ice cream. Makes 9 servings.

When a sudden urge to eat a doughnut strikes, and not one is in the house, you will find doughnuts made from Ranch House Baking mix satisfying. The plain cake doughnuts are quickly made from a rich biscuit-like dough. Roll, cut out doughnuts, quickly fry, and they are ready to eat while still warm. The potato doughnuts are made with yeast and commercial potato flakes. Make a batch of Lemon Potato Doughnuts, dipped in Lemon Honey Glaze. They are sure to please, with requests for more. If you are in a hurry and don't wish to bother with heating shortening or cooking oil, select one of the baked doughnut recipes. Roll out dough, and cut out doughnuts. After baking, the doughnuts are richly coated in a melted butter mixture, then dipped in a sugar mixture. Eat while warm, or cold and crisp straight from the refrigerator for a quick snack.

Leftover doughnuts may be stored in the refrigerator 2 or 3 days, or well wrapped in plastic wrap and stored in freezer up to 1 week.

To reheat doughnuts, thaw first if frozen. Place 4 thickness of waxed paper in center of a length of foil large enough to wrap doughnuts. Place doughnuts on waxed paper. Bring foil up around doughnuts, overlapping at top. Close ends of foil. Place package in baking pan. Heat in oven at 200° until warm, about 12 minutes.

COATING
3/4 cup sugar
1/4 cup butter
1/4 cup Vegetable shortening

DOUGH
2 3/4 cup Ranch House Baking Mix
1/2 cup sugar
2 1/2 tbsp cocoa
1/8 tsp baking soda
2 tbsp Vegetable shortening
1/2 cup buttermilk
1 egg yolk
1/2 tsp vanilla extract

COATING: Place sugar in small shallow bowl; set aside. Melt butter and shortening in small saucepan over low heat. Let stand on burner with heat off.

DOUGH: Place baking mix into medium bowl; stir in sugar, cocoa and baking soda. Cut in shortening with a pastry blender until coarse particles form. Beat buttermilk, egg yolk and vanilla in small bowl at low speed just until blended. Add to baking mix, stir quickly with a fork until barely mixed. If dough seems a little stiff add about 1 to 1 1/2 tablespoons buttermilk, stir quickly until a soft dough forms; let stand 5 minutes. With a rubber spatula remove dough to a floured surface. With floured hands round up into a ball. Lightly coat with flour, knead lightly 8 times.

Pat out with floured palm of hand or roll dough 3/4-inch thick. Cut with floured 2 1/2-inch doughnut cutter. Carefully lift away trimmings, then place doughnuts on a greased baking sheet about 2 1/2 inches apart. Gather up trimmings, lay on top of each other then lightly press together. Pat out dough, cut out doughnuts, remove to baking sheet.

Bake at 400° 12 minutes. Cool doughnuts 5 minutes, then dip into melted butter mixture, coating both sides. Roll in sugar coating until all surfaces are well covered. Place back on baking sheet. Serve warm. Makes 8 doughnuts.

NOTE: Store leftover doughnuts in refrigerator or freezer. To reheat, let come to room temperature. Place 4 thickness of waxed paper in center of a length of foil large enough to wrap doughnuts. Place doughnuts on waxed paper; wrap in foil. Place in baking pan. Heat in oven 200° until warm, about 12 minutes.

CINNAMON BAKED DOUGHNUTS

COATING
3/4 cup sugar
2 1/2 tsp cinnamon
1/4 cups butter
1/4 cup vegetable shortening

DOUGH
2 3/4 cups Ranch House Baking mix
1/3 cups sugar
1 1/4 tsp cinnamon
1/4 tsp each nutmeg and allspice
2 tbsp butter, softened
1/2 cup buttermilk
1 egg yolk

COATING: Combine sugar and cinnamon in small shallow bowl; set aside. Melt butter and shortening in small saucepan over low heat. Let stand on burner with heat off.

DOUGH: Place baking mix into medium bowl; stir in sugar and spices. Cut in butter with a pastry blender until coarse particles form. Beat buttermilk and egg yolk in small bowl at low speed just until blended. Add to baking mix, stir quickly with a fork until barely mixed. If dough seems a little stiff add about 1 to 1 1/2 tablespoons buttermilk, stir quickly until a soft dough forms; let stand 5 minutes. With a rubber spatula remove dough to a floured surface. With floured hands round up into a ball. Lightly coat with flour, knead lightly 8 times. Pat out with floured palm of hand or roll dough 3/4 inch thick. Cut with floured 2 1/2 - inch dough- nut cutter. Carefully lift away trimmings, then place doughnuts on a greased baking sheet about 2 1/2 inches apart. Gather up trimmings, lay on top of each other then lightly press together. Pat out dough, cut out doughnuts, remove to baking sheet.

Bake at 400° 12 minutes. Cool doughnuts 5 minutes, then dip into melted butter mixture, coating both sides. Roll in sugar coating until all surfaces are well covered. Place back on baking sheet. Serve warm. Makes 8 doughnuts.

NOTE: Store leftover doughnuts in refrigerator 2 or 3 days, or wrap well in plastic wrap and freeze 3 months. To re- heat, thaw first if frozen. Place 4 thick- ness of waxed paper in center of a length of foil large enough to wrap doughnuts. Place doughnuts on waxed paper; wrap in foil. Place in baking pan. Heat in oven 200° until warm, about 12 minutes.

COATING
1/2 cup sugar
1/3 cup ground coconut, pk'd
1/4 cup butter, unsalted
1/4 cup vegetable shortening

DOUGH
2 3/4 cups Ranch House Baking mix
1/3 cup ground coconut, pk'd
1/3 cup brown sugar, pk'd
1/4 tsp each cinnamon and nutmeg
2 tbsp butter, softened
1/2 cup buttermilk
1 egg yolk
1/2 tsp coconut extract

COATING: Combine sugar and ground coconut in small shallow bowl; set aside. Melt unsalted butter and shortening in small saucepan over low heat. Let stand on burner with heat off.

DOUGH: Place baking mix into medium bowl; stir in ground coconut, brown sugar and spices. Cut in butter with a pastry blender until coarse particles form. Beat buttermilk, egg yolk and extract in small bowl at low speed just until blended. Add to baking mix, stir quickly with a fork until barely mixed. If dough seems a little stiff add about 1 to 1 1/2 tablespoons buttermilk; stir quickly until a soft dough forms; let stand 5 minutes. With a rubber spatula remove dough to a floured surface. With floured hands round up into a ball. Lightly coat with flour, knead lightly 8 times. Pat out with floured palm of hand or roll dough 3/4- inch thick. Cut with floured 2 1/2- inch doughnut cutter. Carefully lift away trimmings, then place doughnuts on a greased baking sheet about 2 1/2 inches apart. Gather up trimmings, lay on top of each other then lightly press together. Pat out dough, cut out doughnuts, remove to baking sheet.

Bake at 400° 12 minutes. Cool doughnuts 5 minutes, then dip into melted butter mixture, coating both sides. Roll in sugar coating until all surfaces are well covered. Place back on baking sheet. Serve warm. Makes 8 doughnuts.

NOTE: Store leftover doughnuts in refrigerator or freezer. To reheat, let come to room temperature. Place 4 thickness of waxed paper in center of a length of foil large enough to wrap doughnuts. Place doughnuts on waxed paper; wrap in foil. Place in baking pan. Heat in oven 200° until warm, about 12 minutes.

LEMON BAKED DOUGHNUTS

COATING
3/4 cups sugar
rind of 1 lemon
1/4 cups butter
1/4 cup vegetable shortening

DOUGH
2 3/4 cups Ranch House Baking mix
6 tbsp sugar
2 tbsp butter, softened
rind of 1 lemon
7 tbsp buttermilk (1/2 cup less 1 tbsp)
1 tbsp lemon juice
1 egg yolk
1/4 tsp lemon extract

COATING: Place sugar in small shallow bowl. Grate lemon rind over sugar. Stir with fork until well blended; set aside. Melt butter and shortening in small saucepan over low heat. Let stand on burner with heat off.

DOUGH: Place baking mix into medium bowl; stir in sugar. Cut in butter with a pastry blender until coarse particles form. Grate lemon rind over mixture. Beat buttermilk, lemon juice, egg yolk and extract in small bowl at low speed just until blended. Add to baking mix, stir quickly with a fork until barely mixed. If dough seems a little stiff add about 1 to 1 1/3 tablespoons buttermilk, stir quickly until a soft dough forms; let stand 5 minutes. With a rubber spatula remove dough to a floured surface. With floured hands round up into a ball. Lightly

coat with flour, knead lightly 8 times. Pat
out with floured palm of hand or roll dough 3/4-
inch thick. Cut with floured 2½-inch doughnut
cutter. Carefully lift away trimmings, then place
doughnuts on a greased baking sheet about 2½
inches apart. Gather up trimmings, lay on top
of each other then lightly press together. Pat out
dough, cut out doughnuts, remove to baking
sheet.

Bake at 400° 12 minutes. Cool doughnuts
5 minutes, then dip into melted butter mixture,
coating both sides. Roll in sugar coating
until all surfaces are well covered. Place
back on baking sheet. Serve warm. makes
8 doughnuts.

NOTE: Store leftover doughnuts in refrigerator
or freezer. To reheat, let come to room temperature. Place 4 thickness of waxed paper in
center of a length of foil large enough to wrap
doughnuts. Place doughnuts on waxed paper;
wrap in foil. Place in baking pan. Heat in
oven 300° until warm, about 12 minutes.

COATING

3/4 cups sugar
1 1/2 tsp Orange flavored instant breakfast drink powder
1/4 cups butter
1/4 cup Vegetable shortening

DOUGH

2 3/4 cups Ranch House Baking mix
1/3 cup sugar
2 tsp Orange flavored instant breakfast drink powder
2 tbsp butter, softened
rind of 1 orange
1/2 cups buttermilk
1 egg yolk
1/4 tsp orange extract

COATING: Combine sugar and orange powder in small shallow bowl; set aside. Melt butter and shortening in small saucepan over low heat. Let stand on burner with heat off.

DOUGH: Place baking mix into medium bowl; stir in sugar and orange powder. Cut in butter with a pastry blender until coarse particles form. Grate orange rind over mixture. Beat buttermilk, egg yolk and extract in small bowl at low speed just until blended. Add to baking mix, stir quickly with a fork until barely mixed. If dough seems a little stiff add about 1 to 1 1/2 tablespoons buttermilk, stir quickly until a soft dough forms; let stand 5 minutes. With a rubber spatula remove dough to a floured surface. With floured hands round up into a ball. Lightly coat with flour, knead lightly 8 times. Pat out with floured

palm of hand or roll dough 3/4-inch thick.
Cut with floured 2 1/2-inch doughnut cutter.
Carefully lift away trimmings, then place
doughnuts on a greased baking sheet about
2 1/2 inches apart. Gather up trimmings, lay
on top of each other then lightly press together.
Pat out dough, cut out doughnuts, remove
to baking sheet.

Bake at 400° 12 minutes. Cool doughnuts
5 minutes, then dip into melted butter mixture,
coating both sides. Roll in sugar coating
until all surfaces are well covered. Place
back on baking sheet. Serve warm. Makes
8 doughnuts.

NOTE: Store leftover doughnuts in refrigerator
or freezer. To reheat, let come to room temperature. Place 4 thickness of waxed paper in
center of a length of foil large enough to wrap
doughnuts. Place doughnuts on waxed paper,
wrap in foil. Place in baking pan. Heat in
oven 200° until warm, about 12 minutes.

SOUR CREAM BAKED DOUGHNUTS

COATING
3/4 cup sugar
2 tsp cinnamon
1/8 tsp nutmeg
1/4 cup butter
1/4 cup Vegetable shortening

DOUGH
2 3/4 cups Ranch House Baking mix
1/3 cup brown sugar, pkd
1 tsp cinnamon
1/8 tsp each cream of tartar, baking soda
    and ground coriander
1/16 tsp nutmeg
1/16 tsp ground cardamon (optional)
2/3 cups commercial sour cream
1 egg yolk
1 tbsp milk

COATING: Combine sugar and cinnamon
in small shallow bowl; set aside. melt butter
and shortening in small saucepan over low
heat. Let stand on burner with heat off.

DOUGH: Place baking mix into medium
bowl; stir in brown sugar, cinnamon, cream of tartar,
baking soda and remaining spices. Beat sour cream,
egg yolk and milk in small bowl at low speed
just until blended. Add to baking mix, stir
quickly with a fork until barely mixed. If
dough seems a little stiff add about 1 to
1 1/2 Tablespoons milk, stir quickly until
a soft dough forms; let stand 5 minutes.

with a rubber spatula remove dough to a floured surface. With floured hands round up into a ball. Lightly coat with flour, knead lightly 8 times. Pat out with floured palm of hand or roll dough 3/4-inch thick. Cut with floured 2 1/2-inch doughnut cutter. Carefully lift away trimmings, then place doughnuts on a greased baking sheet about 2 1/2 inches apart. Gather up trimmings, lay on top of each other then lightly press together. Pat out dough, cut out doughnuts, remove to baking sheet.

Bake at 400° 12 minutes. Cool doughnuts 5 minutes, then dip into melted butter mixture, coating both sides. Roll in sugar coating until all surfaces are well covered. Place back on baking sheet. Serve warm. Makes 8 doughnuts.

NOTE: Store leftover doughnuts in refrigerator or freezer. To reheat, thaw first if frozen. Place 4 thickness of waxed paper in center of a length of foil large enough to wrap doughnuts. Place doughnuts on waxed paper; wrap in foil. Place in baking pan. Heat in oven 200° until warm, about 12 minutes.

VANILLA BAKED DOUGHNUTS

COATING
3/4 cup sugar
1 1/4 tsp. vanilla extract
1/4 cup butter
1/4 cup vegetable shortening

DOUGH
2 3/4 cups Ranch House Baking mix
1/3 ~~tsp. sugar~~
1/8 tsp. nutmeg
2 tbsp. butter, softened
7 tbsp. milk (1/2 cup less 1 tbsp.)
3/4 tsp. vanilla extract

COATING: Place sugar and vanilla into small shallow bowl. Blend well with a fork. Let dry 3 hours, uncovered, stirring occasionally. (The vanilla-sugar mixture may be prepared in advance; store in a tightly covered jar after drying 3 hours.) Melt butter and shortening in small saucepan over low heat. Let stand on burner with heat off.

DOUGH: Place baking mix into medium bowl; stir in sugar and nutmeg. Cut in butter with a pastry blender until coarse particles form. Beat milk and egg yolk in small bowl at low speed just until blended. Add to baking mix, stir quickly with a fork until barely mixed. If dough seems a little stiff add about 1 to 1 1/2 tablespoons milk, stir quickly until a soft dough forms; let stand 5 minutes. With a rubber spatula remove dough to a floured surface. With floured hands round up into a ball. Lightly coat with flour, knead lightly 8 times. Pat out with floured palm of hand or roll dough 3/4-inch thick. Cut with floured 2 1/2-inch doughnut cutter. Carefully lift away trimmings, then place doughnuts on a greased baking sheet about 2 1/2 inches apart. Gather up trimmings, lay on top of each other then lightly press together. Pat out dough, cut out doughnuts, remove to baking sheet.

Bake at 400° 12 minutes. Cool doughnuts 5 minutes, then dip into melted butter mixture, coating both sides. Roll in sugar coating until all surfaces are well covered. Place back on baking sheet. Serve warm. Makes 8 doughnuts.

NOTE: Store leftover doughnuts in refrigerator or freezer. To reheat, let come to room temperature. Place 4 thickness of waxed paper in center of a length of foil large enough to wrap doughnuts. Place doughnuts on waxed paper; wrap in foil. Place in baking pan. Heat in oven 200° until warm, about 12 minutes.

COATING
1/2 cup sugar
1/3 cup ground walnuts
1/4 cup butter
1/4 cup Vegetable shortening

DOUGH
2 3/4 cups Ranch House Baking mix
1/3 cup ground walnuts
1/3 cup brown sugar, pkd
1/4 tsp nutmeg
2 tbsp Vegetable shortening
1/2 cup buttermilk
1 egg yolk

COATING: Combine sugar and ground walnuts in small shallow bowl; set aside. Melt butter and shortening in small saucepan over low heat. Let stand on burner with heat off.

DOUGH: Place baking mix into medium bowl; stir in ground walnuts, brown sugar and nutmeg. Cut in shortening with a pastry blender until coarse particles form. Beat buttermilk and egg yolk in small bowl at low speed just until blended. Add to baking mix, stir quickly with a fork until barely mixed. If dough seems a little stiff add about 1 to 1 1/2 tablespoons buttermilk, stir quickly until a soft dough forms; let stand 5 minutes. With a rubber spatula remove dough to a floured surface. With floured hands round up into a ball. Lightly coat with flour, knead lightly 8 times. Pat out with floured palm of hand or roll dough 3/4-inch thick. Cut with floured

2 1/2-inch doughnut cutter. Carefully lift away trimmings, then place doughnuts on a greased baking sheet about 2 1/2 inches apart. Gather up trimmings, lay on top of each other then lightly press together. Pat out dough, cut out doughnuts, remove to baking sheet.

Bake at 400° 12 minutes. Cool doughnuts 5 minutes, then dip into melted butter mixture, coating both sides. Roll in sugar coating until all surfaces are well covered. Place back on baking sheet. Serve warm. Makes 8 doughnuts.

NOTE: Store leftover doughnuts in refrigerator or freezer. To reheat, let come to room temperature. Place 4 thickness of waxed paper in center of a length of foil large enough to wrap doughnuts. Place doughnuts on waxed paper; wrap in foil. Place in baking pan. Heat in oven 200° until warm, about 12 minutes.

BUTTERMILK DOUGHNUTS

DOUGH
1 egg
1/4 cup sugar
1/3 cups buttermilk
1/2 tsp vanilla extract
1/8 tsp nutmeg
2 1/2 cups Ranch House Baking mix
Vegetable shortening or cooking oil

CHOCOLATE FROSTING
1/4 cup butter or margarine
1 tbsp light corn syrup
1 tbsp hot water
1/4 cup cocoa
2 cups confectioners' sugar
evaporated milk
1 tsp vanilla extract

While preparing dough, heat vegetable shortening or cooking oil to 360° in a deep-fat fryer, electric skillet or saucepan. If using electric skillet, fill no more than 1/2 full to prevent fat from bubbling over.

DOUGH: Beat egg in medium bowl. Add sugar. Beat at medium speed 3 minutes. Blend in buttermilk, vanilla and nutmeg. Add baking mix, stir quickly with a fork until barely mixed. If dough seems a little stiff add about 1 to 2 tablespoon buttermilk, stir quickly until a soft dough forms; let stand 5 minutes. With a rubber spatula remove dough to a floured surface. With floured hands round up into a ball. Lightly coat with flour, knead lightly 8 times. Pat out with floured palm of hand or roll dough to 1/2-inch thickness. Cut with floured 2 1/2-inch doughnut cutter. Carefully lift away trimmings. Place one doughnut on pancake turner and transfer to hot fat. Leave doughnut on pancake turner until it floats off. Add 2 or 3 more doughnuts. Fry until golden brown around edges, about 1 to 1½ minutes. Turn over with a long-handled fork, being careful not to pierce doughnuts. Fry until golden brown, about 1 to 1½ minutes. With a slotted spoon remove doughnuts to a paper towel lined baking sheet to drain. Gather up trimmings, lay on top of each other then lightly press together. Pat out dough, cut out doughnuts and fry as directed. Cool. Spread tops with frosting. Makes 10 doughnuts.

CHOCOLATE FROSTING: Melt butter in small saucepan over low heat. Stir in syrup and hot water. Remove from heat. Stir in cocoa, blending mixture until smooth. Gradually stir in confectioners' sugar, alternately with a small amount of evaporated milk and the vanilla extract. Beat with a spoon until smooth and creamy.

CHOCOLATE DOUGHNUTS

DOUGH

2 1/2 cups Ranch House Baking mix
1/2 cup sugar
3 tbsp cocoa
1 egg, well beaten
1/3 cup milk
vegetable shortening or cooking oil

CHOCOLATE GLAZE

1/3 cup butter or margarine
3-oz (3 sqs) semi-sweet chocolate
2 cups confectioners' sugar
2 tbsp warm water
1 1/2 tsp vanilla extract

While preparing dough, heat vegetable shortening or cooking oil to 360° in a deep-fat fryer, electric skillet or saucepan. If using electric skillet, fill no more than 1/2 full to prevent fat from bubbling over.

DOUGH: Place baking mix into medium bowl; stir in sugar and cocoa with a pastry blender until well mixed. Combine egg and milk. Stir quickly into baking mix with a fork until barely mixed. If dough seems a little stiff add about 1 to 2 tablespoons milk, stir quickly until a soft dough forms; let stand 5 minutes. With a rubber spatula remove dough to a floured surface. With floured hands round up into a ball. Lightly coat with flour, knead lightly 8 times. Pat out with floured palm of hand or roll dough to 1/2-inch thickness. Cut with floured 2 1/2-inch doughnut cutter. Carefully lift away trimmings. Place one doughnut on pancake turner and transfer to hot fat. Leave doughnut on pancake turner until it floats off. Add 2 or 3 more doughnuts. Fry until golden brown around edges, about 1 to 1½ minutes. Turn over with a long-handled fork, being careful not to pierce doughnuts. Fry until golden brown, about 1 to 1½ minutes. With a slotted spoon remove doughnuts to a paper towel lined baking sheet to drain. Gather up trimmings, lay on top of each other then lightly press together. Pat out dough, cut out doughnuts and fry as directed. Cool doughnuts, then dip into warm glaze, coating both sides. Place on rack over waxed paper. Let stand 2 hours until glaze sets. Makes 10 doughnuts.

CHOCOLATE GLAZE: Melt butter in small saucepan over low heat. Add chocolate, stir until melted. Remove from heat. Gradually stir in 2 cups confectioners' sugar, warm water and vanilla. Beat with spoon until smooth and creamy. Gradually stir in enough warm water to make a thin glaze. If mixture starts to thicken before glazing doughnuts is completed, place saucepan over low heat. Stir until glaze is lukewarm and thins to proper consistency. Makes enough glaze to coat both sides of 10 doughnuts. If you wish to coat only the tops of doughnuts, make ½ of the glaze.

PLAIN DOUGHNUTS

2 1/2 cups Ranch House Baking Mix
1/4 cup sugar
1/2 tsp cinnamon
1/4 tsp nutmeg
1 egg, well beaten
1/3 cups milk
Vegetable shortening or cooking oil
sifted confectioners' sugar or cinnamon sugar

While preparing dough, heat vegetable shortening or cooking oil to 360° in a deep-fat fryer, electric skillet or saucepan. If using electric skillet, fill no more than 1/2 full to prevent fat from bubbling over.

DOUGH: Place baking mix into medium bowl; stir in sugar and spices. Combine egg and milk. Stir quickly into baking mix with a fork until barely mixed. If dough seems a little stiff add about 1 to 2 tablespoons milk; stir quickly until a soft dough forms; let stand 5 minutes. With a rubber spatula remove dough to a floured surface. With floured hands round up into a ball. Lightly coat with flour, knead lightly 8 times. Pat out with floured palm of hand or roll dough to 1/2-inch thickness. Cut with floured 2 1/2-inch doughnut cutter. Carefully lift away trimmings. Place one doughnut on pancake turner and transfer to hot fat. Leave doughnut on pancake turner until it floats off. Add 2 or 3 more doughnuts. Fry until golden brown around edges, about

1 to 1 1/2 minutes. Turn over with a long-handled fork, being careful not to pierce doughnuts. Fry until golden brown, about 1 to 1 1/2 minutes. With a slotted spoon remove doughnuts to a paper towel lined baking sheet to drain. Gather up trimmings, lay on top of each other then lightly press together. Pat out dough, cut out doughnuts and fry as directed. While still warm roll doughnuts in confectioner's sugar or 1/2 cup granulated sugar blended with 3/4 teaspoon cinnamon. Makes 10 doughnuts.

MAPLE NUT DOUGHNUTS

DOUGH
1 egg
1/4 cup brown sugar, pkd
1/3 cup milk
1/2 tsp maple extract
2 1/2 cups Ranch House Baking mix
Vegetable shortening or cooking oil

MAPLE FROSTING
6 tbsp butter, softened
1 3/4 cups confectioners' sugar
2 tsp maple extract
milk
3/4 cup finely chopped walnuts

While preparing dough, heat vegetable shortening or cooking oil to 360° in a deep-fat fryer, electric skillet or saucepan. If using electric skillet, fill no more than 1/2 full to prevent fat from bubbling over.

DOUGH: Beat egg in medium bowl. Add brown sugar. Beat at medium speed 3 minutes. Blend in milk and maple extract. Add baking mix, stir quickly with a fork until barely mixed. If dough seems a little stiff add about 1 to 2 tablespoons milk, stir quickly until a soft dough forms; let stand 5 minutes. With a rubber spatula remove dough to a floured surface. With floured hands round up into a ball. Lightly coat with flour, knead lightly 8 times. Pat out with floured palm of hand or roll dough to 1/2-inch thickness. Cut with floured 2 1/2-inch doughnut cutter. Carefully lift away trimmings. Place one doughnut on pancake turner and transfer to hot fat. Leave doughnut on pancake turner until it floats off. Add 2 or 3 more doughnuts. Fry until golden brown around edges, about 1 to 1 1/2 minutes. Turn over with a long-handled fork, being careful not to pierce doughnuts. Fry until golden brown, about 1 to 1 1/2 minutes. With a slotted spoon remove doughnuts to a paper towel lined baking sheet to drain. Gather up trimmings, lay on top of each other then lightly press together. Pat out dough, cut out doughnuts and fry as directed. Cool. Spread tops with frosting, then dip tops into chopped walnuts. Makes 10 doughnuts.

MAPLE FROSTING: Place butter into small bowl. Gradually stir in confectioners' sugar, alternately with the maple extract and just enough milk to make a smooth creamy frosting.

LEMON POTATO DOUGHNUTS

DOUGH

⅓ cup milk
2 tbsp cold water
⅓ cup potato flakes
1 pkg plus 1 tsp active dry yeast
2 tsp sugar
3 tbsp warm water
1 egg, beaten
3 tbsp sugar
1 tbsp each honey and lemon juice
rind of 1 lemon
3 to 3 ¼ cups Ranch House Baking mix
Vegetable shortening or cooking oil

LEMON HONEY GLAZE

1 ¼ tsp unflavored gelatine
2 tbsp lemon juice
6 tbsp water
6 tbsp sugar
½ of a cinnamon stick
1 whole clove
6 tbsp honey
2 tbsp butter or margarine

DOUGH: Scald milk in small saucepan over low heat. Remove from heat; stir in cold water, then stir in potato flakes. Let stand 2 minutes; whip with a fork until smooth. Cool.

Stir together yeast, 2 teaspoons sugar and warm water in medium bowl; let stand until bubbly, 5 to 10 minutes. Stir in potato mixture, beaten egg, sugar, honey and lemon juice. Grate lemon rind over mixture. Gradually stir in 3 cups of the baking mix with a spoon. Continue mixing until dough leaves sides of bowl and forms a ball. Knead in bowl 2 minutes. If dough sticks to fingers, stir in 2 to 4 tablespoons of the remaining baking mix; knead until smooth. Cover loosely and let rise in a warm place until doubled, about 1 ½ hours. Punch dough down, knead in bowl 1 minute. Transfer to a floured surface.

Roll out to 1/2-inch thickness. Cut with floured 2 1/2-inch doughnut cutter. Carefully lift away trimmings. Place doughnuts on lightly oiled 4 1/2-squares of foil. Transfer to a large baking sheet. Gather up trimmings; knead until smooth. Roll dough, cut out doughnuts. Let rise until doubled, about 1 1/2 hours.

Heat vegetable shortening or cooking oil to 360° in a deep-fat fryer, electric skillet or saucepan. If using electric skillet, fill no more than 1/2 full to prevent fat from bubbling over. Place one doughnut with foil on pancake turner and transfer to hot fat. Remove foil with tongs. Add 2 or 3 more doughnuts. Fry until golden brown around edges, about 1 to 1 1/2 minutes. Turn over with a long-handled fork, being careful not to pierce doughnuts. Fry until golden, about 1 to 1 1/2 minutes. With slotted spoon remove doughnuts to a paper towel lined baking sheet to drain. Cool. Dip doughnuts into warm glaze, coating both sides. Place on rack over waxed paper. Let stand 2 1/2 hours until glaze sets. Makes 1 dozen doughnuts.

LEMON HONEY GLAZE: Soften gelatine in lemon juice in a small custard cup. Combine water, sugar, cinnamon stick and clove in small saucepan. Bring to boiling over medium heat. Lower heat until mixture is simmering. Cook, uncovered, 3 minutes. Stir in honey, butter and gelatine mixture. Continue simmering 2 minutes. Remove from heat. Cover sauce-pan; cool glaze 20 minutes. Remove cinnamon and clove; stir well before glazing doughnuts.

POTATO DOUGHNUTS

Dough

1/3 cup milk
2 tbsp cold water
1/3 cup potato flakes
1 pkg plus 1 tsp active dry yeast
2 tsp sugar
1/4 cup warm water
1 egg, beaten
1/4 cup sugar
3 to 3 1/4 cups Ranch House Baking Mix
Vegetable shortening or cooking oil

COATING

1/2 cup sugar
1 tsp cinnamon

DOUGH: Scald milk in small saucepan over low heat. Remove from heat; stir in cold water, then stir in potato flakes. Let stand 2 minutes; whip with a fork until smooth. Cool.

Stir together yeast, 2 teaspoons sugar and warm water in medium bowl; let stand until bubbly, 5 to 10 minutes. Stir in potato mixture, beaten egg and sugar. Gradually stir in 3 cups of the baking mix with a spoon. Continue mixing until dough leaves sides of bowl and forms a ball. Knead in bowl 2 minutes. If dough sticks to fingers, stir in 2 to 4 tablespoons of the remaining baking mix; knead until smooth. Cover loosely and let rise in a warm place until doubled, about 1 1/2 hours. Punch dough down, knead in bowl 1 minute. Transfer to a floured surface. Roll out to 1/2-inch thickness. Cut with floured 2 1/2-inch doughnut cutter. Carefully lift away trimmings. Place doughnuts on lightly oiled 4 1/2-inch squares of foil. Transfer to a large baking sheet. Gather up trimmings; knead until smooth. Roll dough, cut out doughnuts. Let rise until doubled, about 1 1/2 hours.

Heat vegetable shortening or cooking oil to 360° in a deep-fat fryer, electric skillet or saucepan. If using electric skillet, fill no more than 1/2 full to prevent fat from bubbling over. Place one doughnut with foil on pancake turner and transfer to hot fat. Remove foil with tongs. Add 2 or 3 more doughnuts. Fry until golden brown around edges, about 1 to 1 1/2 minutes. Turn over with a long-handled fork, being careful not to pierce doughnuts. Fry until golden, about 1 to 1 1/2 minutes. With a slotted spoon remove doughnuts to a paper towel lined baking sheet to drain. While still warm roll in sugar coating. Makes 1 dozen doughnuts.

COATING: Place sugar and cinnamon in small bowl. Stir with fork until well blended.

VANILLA POTATO DOUGHNUTS

DOUGH
1/3 cup milk
2 tbsp cold water
1/3 cups potato flakes
1 pkg plus 1 tsp active dry yeast
2 tsp sugar
1/4 cup warm water
1 egg, beaten
1/4 cup sugar
2 tsp vanilla extract
1/4 tsp nutmeg
1/8 tsp mace
3 to 3 1/4 cups R and House Baking mix
Vegetable shortening or cooking oil

VANILLA HONEY GLAZE
1 tsp unflavored gelatine
2 tbsp cold water
1/4 cup hot water
1/4 cup honey
3 tbsp butter or margarine, softened
1 tsp vanilla extract
2 to 2 1/4 cups confectioners' sugar

DOUGH: Scald milk in small saucepan over low heat. Remove from heat; stir in cold water, then stir in potato flakes. Let stand 2 minutes; whip with a fork until smooth. Cool.

Stir together yeast, 2 teaspoons sugar and warm water in medium bowl; let stand until bubbly, 5 to 10 minutes. Stir in potato mixture, beaten egg, sugar, vanilla and spices. Gradually stir in 3 cups of the baking mix with a spoon. Continue mixing until dough leaves sides of bowl and forms a ball. Knead in bowl 2 minutes. If dough sticks to fingers, stir in 2 to 4 tablespoons of the remaining

baking mix; Knead until smooth. Cover loosely 409
and let rise in a warm place until doubled, about
1 1/2 hours. Punch dough down, Knead in bowl
1 minute. Transfer to a floured surface. Roll
out to 1/2-inch thickness. Cut with floured 2 1/2-
inch doughnut cutter. Carefully lift away trimmings.
Place doughnuts on lightly oiled 4 1/2-inch squares
of foil. Transfer to a large baking sheet. Gather up
trimmings; Knead until smooth. Roll dough, cut
out doughnuts. Let rise until doubled, about 1 1/2
hours.

Heat vegetable shortening or cooking oil to
360° in a deep-fat fryer, electric skillet or
saucepan. If using electric skillet, fill no more
than 1/2 full to prevent fat from bubbling over.
Place one doughnut with foil on pancake turner
and transfer to hot fat. Remove foil with tongs.
Add 2 or 3 more doughnuts. Fry until golden
brown around edges, about 1 to 1 1/2 minutes. Turn
over with a long-handled fork, being careful not
to pierce doughnuts. Fry until golden, about 1 to
1 1/2 minutes. With a slotted spoon remove doughnuts to a paper towel lined baking sheet to drain.
Cool. Dip doughnuts into warm glaze, coating
both sides. Place on rack over waxed paper.
Let stand 2 hours until glaze sets. Makes 1
dozen doughnuts.

VANILLA HONEY GLAZE: Soften gelatin in
water in a small custard cup. Combine hot water
and honey in small saucepan. Bring to boiling
over medium heat. Remove from heat. Stir in
gelatine until dissolved. Stir in butter and vanilla.
Gradually beat in 2 cups of the confectioners'
sugar at low speed. If glaze is too thin,
gradually beat in remaining confectioners' sugar.

DUMPLINGS

Making good dumplings can be the nemesis of many a cook, even experienced ones. For the inexperienced cook, turning out a presentable dumpling can be frustrating and baffling. Either they turn out dense and rubbery, or they disintegrate into a soggy mess. The consistency of the dough must be just right to turn out nice fluffy drop dumplings. The dough should be the consistency of drop biscuit dough. If too soft it will spread out and break up as it cooks. Once the dough is dropped into the boiling stew, the heat must be lowered until the liquid is simmering. Too high heat will also contribute to dumplings breaking up. When you are ready to drop the dumplings into the stew, first dip the tablespoon into the hot liquid, then into dough. This will help the dough slide off the spoon. Drop on top of a piece of meat or vegetable if possible. Cook the dumplings as directed in the recipe. Remove to a serving platter with a slotted spoon. Serve immediately.

Strip dumplings are made with a soft dough just firm enough to roll out easily, as in making regular biscuits. The dough is cut into strips, then dropped into gently boiling broth, soup or stew. The heat is then lowered until liquid is simmering. Proceed to cook the dumplings as directed in recipe. Strip dumplings don't break up as readily as drop dumplings, an added advantage if you wish to make dumplings to serve with plain broth.

BUTTERMILK DUMPLINGS

1 1/2 cups Ranch House Baking mix
1/2 cup buttermilk

Place baking mix into small bowl.
Add buttermilk, stir quickly with a fork
until a soft drop dough forms; let
stand 5 minutes. Dip a tablespoon into
boiling stew, then into dough. Scoop
up heaping spoonfuls, drop on top
of meat in 5 equal portions. Cook,
uncovered, over low heat 8 minutes.
Cover, cook 8 minutes longer. Makes
5 dumplings.

BUTTERMILK EGG DUMPLINGS

1 egg
1/4 cups buttermilk
1 1/4 cups Ranch House Baking mix

Beat egg in small bowl. Blend in buttermilk. Add baking mix, stir quickly with a fork until a soft drop dough forms; let stand 5 minutes. Dip a tablespoon into boiling stew, then into dough. Scoop up heaping spoonfuls, drop on top of meat in 4 equal portions. Cook, uncovered, over low heat 8 minutes. Cover, cook 8 minutes longer. Makes 4 large dumplings.

CORNMEAL DUMPLINGS

413

1 3/4 cups Ranch House Baking Mix
1/2 cup Yellow cornmeal
1/2 tsp baking powder
1/4 tsp sugar
1/8 tsp salt
3/4 cup milk

Place baking mix into medium bowl. Stir in cornmeal, baking powder, sugar and salt with a pastry blender until well mixed. Add milk, stir quickly with a fork until a soft drop dough forms; let stand 5 minutes. Dip a tablespoon into boiling stew, then into dough. Scoop up heaping spoonfuls, drop on top of meat in 6 equal portions. Cook, uncovered, over low heat 8 minutes. Cover, cook 8 minutes longer. Makes 6 large dumplings.

DUMPLINGS (BASIC)

1 ½ cups Ranch House Baking Mix
½ cup milk

Place baking mix into small bowl. Add milk, stir quickly with a fork until a soft drop dough forms; let stand 5 minutes. Dip a tablespoon into boiling stew, then into dough. Scoop up heaping spoonfuls, drop on top of meat in 5 equal portions. Cook, uncovered, over low heat 8 minutes. Cover, cook 8 minutes longer. Makes 5 dumplings.

1 1/4 cups Ranch House Baking mix
2 tbsp grated Parmesan cheese
1/4 tsp basil leaves, crumbled
1/8 tsp oregano leaves, crumbled
1 egg
1/4 cup milk

Place baking mix into small bowl. Stir in grated cheese, basil and oregano. Beat egg in small bowl. Blend in milk. Add to baking mix, stir quickly with a fork until a soft drop dough forms; let stand 5 minutes. Dip a tablespoon into boiling stew, then into dough. Scoop up heaping spoonfuls, drop on top of meat in 4 equal portions. Cook, uncovered, over low heat 8 minutes. Cover, cook 8 minutes longer. Makes 4 large dumplings.

PAPRIKA DUMPLINGS

1 cup Ranch House Baking mix
1/4 cup white cornmeal
2 tbsp grated Parmesan cheese
1/2 tsp paprika
1/4 tsp baking powder
1/8 tsp each baking soda, salt and sugar
1 egg
1/4 cup buttermilk

Place baking mix into small bowl. Stir in cornmeal, grated cheese, paprika, baking powder, baking soda, salt and sugar with a pastry blender until well mixed. Beat egg in small bowl. Blend in buttermilk. Add to baking mix, stir quickly with a fork until a soft drop dough forms; let stand 5 minutes. Dip a tablespoon into boiling stew, then into dough. Scoop up heaping spoonfuls, drop on top of meat in 4 equal portions. Cook, uncovered, over low heat 8 minutes. Cover, cook 8 minutes longer. Makes 4 large dumplings.

PARSLEY DUMPLINGS

1 cup Ranch House Baking mix
1/4 cup yellow cornmeal
1/8 tsp each baking soda, salt and sugar
1 egg
1/4 cup buttermilk
1/2 tbsp dry parsley flakes, crumbled

Place baking mix into small bowl. Stir in cornmeal, baking soda, salt and sugar with a pastry blender until well mixed. Beat egg in small bowl. Blend in buttermilk. Stir in parsley flakes with a fork. Add to baking mix, stir quickly with a fork until a soft drop dough forms; let stand 5 minutes. Dip a tablespoon into boiling stew, then into dough. Scoop up heaping spoonfuls, drop on top of meat in 4 equal portions. Cook, uncovered, over low heat 8 minutes. Cover, cook 8 minutes longer. Makes 4 large dumplings.

STEAMED PORK DUMPLINGS

FILLING
1 tbsp butter
2 green onions, finely sliced
1 tbsp catsup
2 tsp soy sauce
1 1/2 tsp Worcestershire sauce
1 1/2 tsp dark molasses
1/8 tsp each ground ginger, dry mustard, pepper and garlic
    powder
1 1/4 cups chopped leftover roast pork

DOUGH
1 1/2 tsp active dry yeast
1/2 tsp sugar
1/4 cup warm water
2 1/2 tbsp evaporated milk
1 1/2 cups Ranch House Baking Mix

FILLING: Melt butter in a small skillet over low-to-medium heat. Add green onions. Cook and stir 2 minutes. Remove from heat. Stir in remaining ingredients, except meat. Add chopped pork, stir until well mixed; set aside.

DOUGH: Stir together yeast, sugar and warm water in medium bowl. Let stand until bubbly, 5 to 10 minutes. Stir in evaporated milk. Gradually stir in baking mix with a spoon. Continue mixing until a soft spongy dough forms, about 2 minutes. Transfer to a floured surface. Lightly coat with flour. Divide into 8 equal pieces; lightly coat with flour. Roll into smooth balls between palms of hands. Pat out one ball of dough to a 4 3/4-inch circle, making edges thin. Place 2 rounded tablespoon filling in center of circle. Gather edges together, pinch seams to seal. Repeat with remaining dough and filling. Coat steamer rack with non-stick vegetable spray. Pour boiling water into steamer until water comes to within 1 1/4 inches from bottom of rack. Place dumplings, seam side down, on steamer rack, allowing room to spread. Cover, steam over gently boiling water until dough is cooked through, about 16 to 17 minutes. Serve with soup, stew or as a side dish. Makes 8 dumplings.

NOTE: For extra light dumplings, line a baking sheet with waxed paper; lightly dust with flour. Place filled dumplings on waxed paper. Let rise in a warm place 1 hour. Steam as directed.

If you don't have a regular steamer, you may use a 9-inch vegetable steamer rack in a Dutch oven. Pour boiling water into Dutch oven, leaving at least 3/4 inch free space from bottom of rack. Steam as directed.

1 1/4 cups Ranch House Baking mix
2 tbsp grated Parmesan cheese
1/4 tsp basil leaves, crumbled
1/8 tsp oregano leaves, crumbled
1/4 cup plus 1 tbsp milk

Place baking mix into small bowl.
Stir in grated cheese, basil and oregano. Add
milk, stir quickly with a fork until barely
mixed. If dough seems a little stiff add
about 1/2 to 3/4 tablespoon milk, stir quickly
until a soft dough forms; let stand 5 minutes.
With a rubber spatula remove dough to a
floured surface. With floured hands round
up into a ball. Lightly coat with flour,
knead lightly 8 times. Pat out with floured
hand to a 4-inch square. Cut crosswise
in half, then cut through center of dough
lengthwise to make four 2-inch squares.
Cut squares lengthwise through center to
make 8 strips. Drop into boiling stew,
soup or broth. Cook, uncovered, over
low heat 7 minutes. Cover, cook 5
minutes longer. Makes 8 strip dumplings.

1 1/4 cups Ranch House Baking Mix
3/4 tsp chili powder
1/8 tsp each cumin powder and coriander powder
1/4 cup plus 1 tbsp milk

Combine baking mix and spices in small bowl. Add milk, stir quickly with a fork until barely mixed. If dough seems a little stiff add about 1/2 to 3/4 tablespoon milk, stir quickly until a soft dough forms; let stand 5 minutes. With a rubber spatula remove dough to a floured surface. With floured hands round up into a ball. Lightly coat with flour, knead lightly 8 times. Pat out with floured hand to a 4-inch square. Cut crosswise in half, then cut through center of dough lengthwise to make four 2-inch squares. Cut squares lengthwise through through center to make 8 strips. Drop into boiling stew, soup or broth. Cook, uncovered, over low heat 7 minutes. Cover, cook 5 minutes longer. Makes 8 strip dumplings.

PLAIN STRIP DUMPLINGS

1 1/4 cups Ranch House Baking mix
1/4 cup plus 1 tbsp milk (note below)

Place baking mix into small bowl. Add milk, stir quickly with a fork until barely mixed. If dough seems a little stiff add about 1/2 to 3/4 tablespoon milk, stir quickly until a soft dough forms; let stand 5 minutes. With a rubber spatula remove dough to a floured surface. With floured hands round up into a ball. Lightly coat with flour, knead lightly 8 times. Pat out with floured hand to a 4-inch square. Cut crosswise in half, then cut through center of dough lengthwise to make four 2-inch squares. Cut squares lengthwise through center to make 8 strips. Drop into boiling stew, soup or broth. Cook, uncovered, over low heat 7 minutes. Cover, cook 5 minutes longer. Makes 8 strip dumplings.

NOTE: Buttermilk may be substituted for the sweet milk. Increase buttermilk by 1/2 tablespoon.

6 tbsp boiling water
1/8 tsp salt
3 tbsp cold milk
1/3 cups potato flakes
1 1/2 cups R and House Baking mix
2 to 4 tsp milk

Place boiling water and salt into small bowl. Add 3 tablespoons cold milk. Stir in potato flakes. Let stand 2 minutes, then whip with a fork until smooth. Let stand 15 minutes. Add baking mix. Stir with a fork until well mixed and dough softens. Dough will appear to be very dry at first, but with continued mixing it will soften to consistency of biscuit dough. If it is too dry, gradually stir in 2 to 4 teaspoons milk. With a rubber spatula remove dough to a floured surface. With floured hands round up into a ball. Lightly coat with flour, knead lightly 8 times. Pat out with floured hand to a 5-inch square. Cut crosswise in half, then cut through center of dough lengthwise to make four 2 1/2-inch squares. Cut squares lengthwise through center to make 8 strips. Drop into boiling stew, soup or broth. Cook, uncovered, over low heat 7 minutes. Cover, cook 6 minutes longer. Makes 8 strip dumplings.

1 1/2 cups Ranch House Baking Mix
1/3 cup yellow stone ground cornmeal
1 1/2 tbsp each grated Swiss and Parmesan cheese
1/2 tsp each onion powder and sugar
1/8 tsp each salt, baking powder and baking soda
1/2 cup buttermilk
1/4 tsp bottled hot sauce

Combine baking mix, cornmeal, grated cheese,
onion powder, sugar, salt, baking powder and
soda in medium bowl with a pastry blender.
Add buttermilk and hot sauce, stir quickly
with a fork until barely mixed. If dough seems
too dry, quickly stir in about 1 tablespoon water;
let stand 5 minutes. With a rubber spatula remove
dough to a floured surface. With floured hands
round up into a ball. Lightly coat with flour,
knead lightly 8 times. Pat out with floured hand to
a 4 1/2-inch square. Cut crosswise in half, then
cut through center of dough lengthwise to make
four 2 1/4-inch squares. Cut squares lengthwise through center to make 8 strips. Drop
into boiling stew, soup or broth. Cook, uncovered, over low heat 7 minutes. Cover, cook
6 minutes longer. Makes 8 strip dumplings.

Perk up your menus with one of these tempting entrees. The meat and potato people of the house will sooner or later ask for something different to eat. Be ready for them, with a surprise that will please the palate. For two easy-to-prepare entrees that require no pot watching, try Smothered Chicken and "Souper" Baked Chicken. They are baked in a rich gravy, and topped with nicely browned, crusty drop biscuits. For supper with a Spanish flavor, cook a pot of chili. Serve with a Guacamole-topped Tostada salad. When time permits, bake ahead several batches of Entree Puff Shells. They may be frozen for 3 months. For a quick meal, then, reheat and fill with shrimp, ham and cheese, chicken or one of your favorite fillings. If you like stew you will love Oven Beef Burgundy Stew, topped with Drop Biscuit Topping. There are many more interesting entrees to choose from. Prepare them as a special surprise, if appetites begin to lag when the usual fare is served.

ALBONDIGAS SOUP WITH DUMPLINGS

BEEF BROTH
8 cups hot water
2 tbsp instant beef bouillon granules

ALBONDIGAS
3/4 lb lean ground beef
1 egg, beaten
2 1/2 tbsp water
1 1/2 tbsp flour
1/4 tsp each salt, seasoned salt, Old Bay seasoning, thyme leaves, crushed, and basil leaves, crushed

1 recipe MEXICAN STRIP DUMPLINGS (P-421)

BEEF BROTH: Place hot water into Dutch oven or large pot. Stir in bouillon. Bring to boiling over high heat.

ALBONDIGAS: Combine ingredients in medium bowl. Mix until well blended. Dampen hands with cold water. Shape meat mixture into 1-inch balls. Drop into boiling broth. Lower heat until broth is simmering. Cover, cook 20 minutes. Drop in strip dumplings. Simmer, uncovered, 7 minutes; cover and simmer 5 minutes longer. Makes 4 servings.

CHEESE DOGS IN A BASKET

1 recipe YEAST PRESS-IN PASTRY (P-588)
8 hot dogs (1 1-lb pkg)
6-oz Cheddar cheese

PREPARE PASTRY; Transfer to a floured surface. Divide into 8 equal pieces. Lightly coat with flour. Roll into smooth balls between palms of hands; set aside. Make deep slits in hot dogs, cutting almost to the ends. Slice cheese into sticks 1/4 to 1/2-inch wide. Insert into hot hot dogs; set aside. Pat out balls of dough, one at a time, to 5-inch squares on a floured surface. Place one filled hot dog diagonally on pastry. Bring one corner over to 3/4 cover hot dog. Bring opposite corner over to overlap pastry and complete basket. Dampen undersurface of top point. Pinch to seal. Place on a lightly greased baking sheet. Repeat with remaining pastry and hot dogs.

Bake at 325° about 20 minutes until cheese melts and pastry is golden. Makes 8 servings.

NOTE: If a thicker pastry covering for hot dogs is preferred, divide pastry into 6 equal pieces. Use 6 hot dogs and 5-oz Cheddar cheese.

CHILI AND TACOTILLAS

CHILI
1 tbsp olive oil
2 lbs lean ground beef
1 1/2 cups chopped onions
1 16-oz can stewed tomatoes
1 8-oz can tomato sauce
1 6-oz can tomato paste
1 4-oz can chopped green chilies
1/4 cup chili powder
1 tbsp worcestershire sauce
2 tsp instant beef bouillon granules
1 1/2 tsp Old Bay seasoning and Tabasco sauce
1 tsp each cumin powder and ground coriander
3/4 tsp each garlic powder, seasoned salt,
    oregano leaves, crumbled, and paprika
1/2 cup each beer and water
1 small bay leaf

TACOTILLAS
1 1/2 cups Ranch House Baking mix
1 tsp chili powder
1/4 tsp each Old Bay seasoning and cumin powder
1/8 tsp garlic salt
2 tbsp vegetable shortening
1 tsp active dry yeast
1/2 tsp sugar
1/4 cup warm water
1 tbsp evaporated milk
cooking oil for frying

CHILI: Fry ground beef in olive oil in Dutch oven over medium-to-high heat until red color leaves meat, breaking up chunks as it cooks. Spoon off fat. Push meat to one side of pot. Add onions. Fry over low heat until pale golden and tender, about 10 minutes, stirring occasionally. Stir onions into meat. Continue cooking 5 minutes, stirring occasionally. Stir in remaining ingredients. Bring to boiling then lower heat until chili is simmering. Cover. Cook 1 1/2 hours, stirring frequently to prevent scorching. While chili is cooking prepare tacotillas.

TACOTILLAS: Place baking mix into small bowl; stir in spices. Cut in shortening with a pastry blender until coarse particles form; set aside.

Combine yeast, sugar and warm water in a 1-cup measure; let stand until bubbly, 5 to 10 minutes. Add to baking mix along with the evaporated milk. Stir with a spoon until dough leaves the sides of bowl. Continue stirring 2 minutes. Divide into 4 equal portions; using a slightly rounded 1/4 cup measure for each tortilla. Flatten into 3-inch rounds on a piece of waxed paper.

Place into a small waxed paper lined baking pan. Cover with waxed paper. Quick chill in freezer 20 minutes or until firm enough to roll out. Place rounds on a floured surface, one at a time. Lightly coat with flour. Roll out with a floured rolling pin to a 6 1/2-inch circle. Fry in 1 teaspoon cooking oil in 7-inch skillet over medium heat until golden brown, about 2 to 3 minutes. Turn, fry until golden, about 2 minutes. Remove to center of a 24-inch length of foil. Fry remaining tortillas, using 1 teaspoon oil for each. Stack, then wrap in foil. Dampen 3 paper towels, then place on the bottom of a baking pan. Place package of tortillas on the damp towels. Keep warm in 180° oven until serving time. Serve with the chili. Makes 4 servings.

NOTE: Canned Mexican style beans may be added to the chili if desired. Use one 15-oz can of beans for 2 cups chili.

CHILI AND TOSTADOS

1 recipe CHILI (P-428)
1 recipe TACO TILLAS (P-428)
1 1/2 15-oz cans mexican style beans

GUACAMOLE
2 large ripe avocados
2 tbsp grated onion
1 tbsp lemon juice
1/4 tsp each garlic powder, garlic salt or 1 Old Bay seasoning
1 tbsp mayonnaise

TOSTADA TOPPING
2 cups chili without beans
1 cup (4 oz) grated Jack cheese
shredded lettuce
2 medium tomatoes, cut into 1/2-inch cubes
6 green onions, minced
1/2 cup commercial Green Goddess salad dressing
1/4 cup cold water

PREPARE CHILI as directed; Remove 2 1/4 cups of the cooked chili to medium saucepan. Continue simmering, uncovered, until very thick, stirring frequently to prevent scorching; set aside. Add beans to remaining chili in Dutch oven; set aside.

GUACAMOLE: Peel avocados; remove pits. mash in medium bowl until fairly smooth. Stir in grated onion, lemon juice and seasonings. Spoon into a 2-cup measure. Carefully spread mayonnaise over top of guacamole to prevent darkening. Cover with plastic wrap. Chill. (Just before serving, stir mayonnaise into guacamole.) makes 2 cups.

TOSTADOS: Prepare tortillas as directed. Fry in oil then transfer to a large baking sheet. arrange in single file. Bake in 325° oven 5 minutes. Turn, continue baking

5 minutes. Reheat chili and beans in Dutch oven over medium heat, and chili in saucepan over low heat, while tocotillas are heating in oven.

Transfer hot tocotillas to 4 large shallow soup bowls or serving plates. Spread 1/2 cup chili without beans over each tocotilla. Layer with 1/4 cup grated cheese, a generous helping shredded lettuce, 1/4 of the tomato cubes and green onions, then another layer of lettuce. Combine salad dressing and cold water in a 1-cup measure. Drizzle 3 tablespoons over each Tostada. Top with 1/2 cup gucamole.

Spoon chili with beans into serving bowls. Top with diced spanish onions if desired. makes 4 servings.

CHIPPED BEEF A LA KING

1 recipe ENTREE BISCUITS (P-20)
3 3-oz pkgs sliced smoked beef
6 tbsp butter or margarine
7 tbsp flour
3 cups hot milk
1/2 tsp onion powder
1/4 tsp pepper

Bake biscuits as directed, while preparing sauce.

Cut beef into narrow strips; set aside. Melt butter in large skillet over low heat. Stir in flour with a fork until well blended. Gradually stir in hot milk. Continue cooking and stirring over medium heat until sauce thickens. Add beef, onion powder and pepper. Cook and stir 2 minutes. If a thinner sauce is desired add more milk.

Separate hot biscuits. Place bottom half on serving plates. Spoon with 1/2 of the creamed beef, dividing evenly. Top with upper half of biscuit. Spoon on remaining creamed beef. Makes 6 servings.

CORN DOGS

3 cups hot water
6 hot dogs
3/4 cup Ranch House Baking mix
1/2 cup yellow cornmeal
1/2 tsp sugar
1/8 tsp salt
1/2 cup plus 1/2 tbsp milk
1 egg, beaten
6 wooden skewers
cooking oil

Bring hot water to boiling in medium saucepan. Add hot dogs. Bring water to boiling again then immediately remove saucepan from heat. Cover; let stand 20 minutes.

Combine baking mix, cornmeal, sugar and salt in small bowl. Add milk and egg. Stir with beaters to dampen, beat at medium speed 20 seconds. Scrape bowl with a rubber spatula, stir 10 turns. Transfer batter to a tall glass, such as used for iced tea. Let stand 10 minutes.

Pour cooking oil into electric skillet or large frying pan until oil reaches half way up sides of pan. Heat to 425°. Remove hot dogs from water. Dry thoroughly with paper towels. Insert skewers in one end, leaving 1 1/2 inches protruding to use as a handle. Dip hot dogs into batter then quickly transfer to hot oil. Fry until lightly browned, about 1 minute. Turn with tongs; fry until lightly browned, about 1 minute. Remove with tongs to a paper towel lined baking sheet to drain. Makes 6 servings.

MEATBALLS
1 egg
1 1/2 lbs lean ground beef
1/2 cup chopped onion
1/2 cup tomato soup, undiluted
1/4 cup cracker crumbs
2 Tsp Prime Choice ~~flavor~~
1/2 Tsp each salt, ~~garlic salt~~, ground coriander
   and worcestershire sauce
1/4 Tsp pepper
1 tbsp olive oil for frying

1 qt commercial Italian sauce

FLORENTINE DUMPLINGS; recipe follows

MEATBALLS: Beat egg in medium bowl. Add remaining ingredients; stir until well mixed. Shape into 10 meatballs. Heat Dutch oven over medium heat. Add olive oil. Fry meatballs until well browned on both sides. Add Italian sauce. Bring to boiling, cover, then lower heat until mixture is simmering. ~~Cook~~ 25 minutes. Dip a tablespoon into hot sauce, then into dumpling dough. Scoop up heaping spoonfuls, drop on top of meatballs in 5 equal portions. Cook dumplings, uncovered,

8 minutes. Cover, cook 8 minutes longer.
makes 5 servings.

FLORENTINE DUMPLINGS: Place 2 cups
Ranch House Baking mix, 3 Tablespoons
grated Parmesan cheese, 1/4 teaspoon basil, crumbled,
and 1/8 teaspoon oregano, crumbled, into medium
bowl. Beat 1 egg in a small bowl; blend
in 1/2 cup buttermilk. Add to baking mix,
stir quickly with a fork until a soft
drop dough forms; let stand 5 minutes.

MEAT LOAF

1 lb lean ground beef
3/4 lb whole hog hot pork sausage, from a 1-lb roll
1/2 cup chopped onions
1/2 cup milk
1/3 cup cracker crumbs
1 egg, beaten
1 tbsp Worcestershire sauce
1 tbsp Prime Choice sauce
1 tsp salt

1 recipe 6 serving size HOT BREAD SQUARES (P-117)

PAN GRAVY

1/4 cup flour
2 tbsp Bisto Gravy mix
6 tbsp butter or margarine
3 cups milk
salt and pepper to taste

MEAT LOAF: Place ground beef into large bowl. Add pork sausage. Let stand 30 minutes to remove chill. Add remaining ingredients. Stir until well mixed. Spoon mixture into a 12 by 7½-inch glass baking dish; shape into meat loaf. Cover dish with foil; set aside. Prepare bread as directed. Place in a greased 13 by 9-inch baking pan to rise. While bread is rising, bake meat loaf at 325° 1 hour. Remove foil; spoon off fat. Continue baking, uncovered, 30 minutes longer. Let cool 20 minutes before slicing. Bake bread as directed while meat loaf is cooling. Prepare gravy while bread is baking.

Cut hot bread into 6 equal portions.

Transfer to serving plates. Spread 2 tablespoons gravy over top of each serving. Top with a slice meat loaf. Spoon with gravy. Serve with mashed potatoes and a green salad for a complete meal. Makes 6 servings.

PAN GRAVY: Combine flour and Bisto in a 1-cup measure. Melt butter in large skillet over low heat. Stir in flour mixture with a fork. Gradually stir in milk. Cook and stir over medium heat until gravy thickens. Stir in salt and pepper to taste.

NOTE: Bisto Gravy mix is available in the gourmet food section of supermarkets. It gives gravy a nicely browned appearance and adds flavor.

1 recipe YEAST PRESS-IN PASTRY (p. 588)

FILLING
½ Tbsp vegatable shortening
½ lb lean ground beef
½ cup frozen chopped onions
3/4 cups hot water
2 Tbsp chopped black olives
2 Tsp chili powder
1 ½ Tsp instant beef bouillon granules
¼ tsp garlic powder
¼ tsp paprika
⅛ Tsp thyme
⅛ Tsp pepper
1 small potato, pared and cut into ½-inch cubes

FILLING: melt shortening in medium
saucepan over medium-to-high heat.
Add ground beef, fry until red color leaves
meat. Stir occasionally to break up the
chunks. Spoon off all but ½ tablespoon fat.
Push meat to one side of pan. Add onions,
sauté over low-to-medium heat until
tender. Stir into meat, cook 5 minutes
longer. Add remaining ingredients, stir
until well mixed. Cover, bring to boiling
over high heat, then lower heat until
broth is simmering. Cook until potatoes
are almost tender, about 22 to 25 minutes.
uncover, cook until liquid has evaporated,

stirring occasionally. Blend potatoes into meat mixture with a potato masher. Cool.

PREPARE PASTRY; transfer to a floured surface. Lightly coat with flour. Divide into 6 equal pieces. Lightly coat with flour. Roll each piece into a smooth ball between palms of hands. Roll out to a 6-inch circle on a floured surface. Spoon 3 1/2 tablespoons of the filling onto one half of the pastry. Spread to within 3/4-inch of edges. Moisten edges with water. Fold unfilled side of pastry over filling. Press edges together to seal, then roll edges back toward filled pastry. Crimp edges with floured tines of fork. Place turnover on a lightly greased baking sheet. Repeat with remaining pastry and filling.

Bake at 350° 15 to 18 minutes until crust is golden brown. Makes 6 servings.

PEPPERONI PIES

440

1 recipe YEAST PRESS-IN PASTRY (P-588)

FILLING
2 3-oz pkgs cream cheese, softened
1 1/2 tbsp sandwich spread
1 1/2 tbsp barbecue sauce
1 1/2 tbsp evaporated milk
1 1/2 cups (6-oz) grated mozzarella cheese
3/4 cup minced pepperoni sausage

PREPARE PASTRY; transfer to a 16-inch length of waxed paper. Pat out to a 6-inch circle, then wrap in the waxed paper. Place in a small baking pan. Quick chill in freezer 30 minutes.

FILLING: Combine cream cheese, sandwich spread, barbecue sauce and evaporated milk in medium bowl. Beat with a spoon until well blended. Fold in grated cheese and pepperoni.

Place chilled pastry on a floured surface. Lightly coat with flour. Roll out to a 12-inch circle. Trim uneven edges. Cut into 6 wedges. Transfer 1 wedge to a large ungreased baking sheet. Spread 1/3 cup filling over dough to within 3/4-inch of edges, slightly mounding in center lengthwise. Form a 1/2-inch rim around edges of pastry, pressing rim slightly inward at an angle to contain filling. Firmly press dough at corners and point of triangle to help keep rim intact during baking. Repeat with remaining wedges. When pan gets too crowded for

for shaping dough, cut out 6-inch wedges of foil. Place dough on foil; fill and shape. Lift foil wedge with pie onto baking sheet. Let pies stand in a warm place 1 hour.

Bake at 350° 18 to 20 minutes until golden brown. Makes 6 pies.

PEPPERONI AND SAUSAGE PIZZA

DOUGH
1 pkg active dry yeast
1 tsp sugar
2/3 cups warm water
2 1/2 to 2 3/4 cups Ranch House Baking Mix

SAUCE
1/2 cups undiluted canned tomato soup
1/4 cups plus 2 tbsp tomato paste
1 tbsp olive oil
1 tbsp hot water
3/4 tsp basil leaves, crumbled
1/4 tsp oregano leaves, crumbled
1/2 tsp onion powder
1/4 tsp garlic powder
1/8 tsp pepper

TOPPING
1/2 lb italian sausage, casings removed
3/4 cup thinly sliced pepperoni
1 cup (4-oz) grated Jack cheese
2 cups (8-oz) grated mozzarella cheese
4 tbsp grated Parmesan cheese, divided
2 tbsp olive oil

DOUGH: Stir together yeast, sugar and warm water in medium bowl; let stand until bubbly, 5 to 10 minutes. Gradually stir in 2 1/2 cups of the baking mix with a spoon. Continue mixing until dough leaves sides of bowl and forms a smooth ball. Knead in bowl 2 minutes. If dough sticks to fingers, stir in enough of the remaining baking mix to form a non-sticky dough; knead until smooth. Cover loosely and let rise in a warm place until doubled, about 1 1/2 hours. While dough is rising, prepare sauce and topping.

SAUCE: Combine ingredients in small bowl with a spoon. Let stand 45 minutes.

TOPPING: Fry sausage in small skillet over medium heat until well browned, breaking up chunks as it cooks. Remove from heat; spoon off fat. Soak up any remaining fat by pressing paper towels over surface. Cool to lukewarm.

Punch dough down; knead in bowl 1 minute. Transfer to a greased on bottom only 14-inch round pizza pan. Press dough with fingers and palm of hand to cover bottom and sides of pan, pressing firmly against sides to anchor. Bake shell at 375° 7 minutes. Cool on rack 10 minutes. Spoon sauce evenly over bottom of shell. Sprinkle with 2 tablespoons of the Parmesan cheese. Sprinkle sausage over sauce, then layer with pepperoni, spacing evenly. Sprinkle with grated jack cheese, then with the mozzarella and remaining parmesan cheese. Drizzle olive oil over topping.

Bake at 375° 15 to 17 minutes until cheese melts and bubbles, and crust is nicely browned. Cool 10 minutes. Makes 3 to 4 servings.

1 recipe YEAST PRESS-IN PASTRY (P-588)
6 hot dogs

POTATO SALAD
2 medium potatoes
6 tbsp salad dressing
3 tbsp commercial sour cream
1/4 cup finely chopped celery
2 small green onions, finely chopped
1 tbsp chopped black olives
1/2 tbsp sweet pickle relish
1 tsp prepared mustard
2 hard-cooked eggs, mashed

PREPARE PASTRY; Transfer to a floured surface. Divide into 6 equal pieces. Lightly coat with flour. Roll into smooth balls between palms of hands. Pat out 1 ball to a 5 1/2-inch square. Split hot dogs lengthwise. Place 1 hot dog on the pastry square diagonally. Spoon a rounded 1/4 cup potato salad onto hot dog. Spread to cover evenly. Bring two corners of pastry together at center of hot dog. Pinch to seal. Place on a lightly greased baking sheet. Repeat with remaining pastry and hot dogs.

Bake at 325° about 25 minutes until pastry is golden brown. Makes 6 servings.

POTATO SALAD: Peel potatoes. Place in medium saucepan. Add 1½ teaspoons salt and water to cover ¾ up sides of potatoes. Bring to boiling over high heat. Lower heat until water is simmering. Cover, cook potatoes until tender. Drain off water. Coarsely mash potatoes. Cool to lukewarm, uncovered. Stir together remaining ingredients in small bowl. Spoon over mashed potatoes. Stir until well mixed. Add salt and pepper to taste.

SAUSAGE TURNOVERS

1 recipe YEAST PRESS-IN PASTRY (p-588)

FILLING

1 1-lb roll whole hog hot pork sausage
½ cup frozen chopped onions, unthawed
3 tbsp commercial dry bread crumbs
1 large egg, beaten

GLAZE

1 egg yolk
1 tbsp milk

FILLING: Remove casing from sausage. Place in large preheated skillet or Dutch oven over low-to-medium heat. Add onions. Fry until meat is lightly browned and onions are tender; stir occasionally. Remove from heat. Spoon off fat. Press paper towels over meat to soak up remaining excess fat. Stir in bread crumbs until well blended. Pour beaten egg over meat mixture, stir until well blended. Let stand until cold, about 1 hour.

PREPARE PASTRY; transfer to a floured surface; lightly coat with flour. Divide into 6 equal pieces. Lightly coat with flour. Roll each piece into a smooth ball between palms of hands. Roll out 1 ball to a 6-inch circle on a floured surface. Spoon 3 tablespoons (lightly packed) filling onto one half of the pastry. Spread to within 3/4-inch of edges. Moisten edges with water. Fold unfilled side of pastry over filling. Press edges together to seal, then roll back toward filling. Crimp rolled edges with floured tines of fork. Place on a lightly greased baking sheet. Repeat with remaining pastry. Lightly brush glaze over turnovers with a pastry brush.

Bake at 350° 15 minutes until golden brown. Makes 6 servings.

GLAZE: Place egg yolk and milk into small custard cup. Stir with a fork until well mixed.

1 recipe 6 serving size HOT BREAD SQUARES (P-117)

MORNAY SAUCE
3 egg yolks
1/4 cup water
1/4 cup butter or margarine
1/4 cup flour
2 cups milk
1 cup (4-oz) grated Swiss cheese
1 tsp Worcestershire sauce
1/2 tsp onion powder
salt to taste

SCRAMBLED EGGS
8 eggs plus 3 whites
1/2 cup milk
1/2 tsp salt
2 tbsp butter or margarine

Prepare and bake bread as directed. Let stand in pan 10 minutes. Cut into 6 equal portions. (30 minutes before placing bread in oven to bake, prepare sauce and scrambled eggs.)

MORNAY SAUCE: Beat egg yolks and water in small bowl at low speed just until blended. Strain into a 1-cup measure; set aside. Melt butter in medium skillet over low heat. Stir in flour with a fork. Remove from heat; gradually stir in 1 cup of the milk. Return to medium heat; gradually stir in remaining 1 cup milk. Cook and stir until sauce thickens. Remove from heat; stir in egg yolks. Return to low heat; cook and stir 1 minute. Add grated cheese, worcestershire and onion powder. Cook and stir until cheese melts and sauce is smooth. Add salt to taste. Cover pan. Let stand on burner with heat off. (Reheat just before serving if sauce cools.)

SCRAMBLED EGGS: Beat eggs, milk and salt in medium bowl until blended. Melt butter in large skillet over low-to-medium heat. Pour in eggs. Slowly scrape bottom and sides of pan with a small metal spatula or fork as eggs begin to set. Cook just until egg is of desired firmness. Remove pan from heat.

Place hot bread on serving plates. Top with scrambled eggs. Spoon with sauce. Makes 6 servings.

ALBONDIGAS
1 1/2 lbs lean ground beef
1 egg, beaten
5 tbsp water
3 tbsp flour
1/2 tsp each crumbled thyme leaves, onion salt,
garlic powder, chili powder, salt and pepper
2 quarts hot water

GRAVY
1 10 3/4-oz can cream of celery soup
1 10 3/4-oz can cream of mushroom soup
1 1/2 cups strained albondigas broth, reserved
1 tbsp cold water
1/8 tsp dry mustard
1 tsp Prime Choice steak sauce
1/2 tsp Worcestershire sauce
1/8 tsp pepper

DROP BISCUIT TOPPING
2 cups Ranch House Baking mix
2/3 cups milk

ALBONDIGAS: Thoroughly blend together ground beef, beaten egg, water, flour and seasonings in medium bowl. Shape into 25 meatballs 1 1/4-inches in diameter. Bring hot water to boiling in large saucepan. Drop in meatballs. Simmer, uncovered, 15 minutes. Remove with a slotted spoon to a 13 by 9-inch baking pan. Pour hot gravy over meatballs. Cover top of pan with foil, leaving 1 1/2-inch free space at long sides to let steam escape.

Bake at 400° 18 minutes. Remove foil.

Dip a tablespoon into hot gravy, then into biscuit dough. Scoop up heaping spoonfuls, drop on top of meatballs in 5 equal portions. Continue baking, uncovered, 22 minutes until biscuits are lightly browned. Makes 5 servings.

GRAVY: Place soup in medium saucepan. Gradually stir in Albondigas broth. Combine cold water and mustard. Add to soup mixture, along with remaining ingredients. Place over medium heat until hot, stirring occasionally.

DROP BISCUIT TOPPING: Place baking mix into medium bowl. Add milk, stir quickly with a fork until a soft dry dough starts to form. If dough seems a little stiff quickly stir in about 1 tablespoon milk, let stand 5 minutes.

BEEF PATTIES

1 egg
1 1/4 lbs lean ground beef
1/2 cup milk
1/4 cup chopped onions
1/4 cup deseeded chopped canned green chilies
1/4 cup yellow cornmeal
3 tbsp cracker crumbs
1/2 tsp each seasoned salt, garlic salt and
    dry mustard
1/8 tsp pepper
1 tbsp vegetable shortening for frying

GRAVY

1 10 1/2-oz can cream of mushroom soup
1 10 1/2-oz can cream of onion soup
1 1/2 cups hot water
1 tsp Worcestershire sauce
2 medium onions
DROP BISCUIT TOPPING; recipe follows

BEEF PATTIES: Beat egg in medium bowl.
Add remaining ingredients; stir until well mixed.
Divide into 4 equal portions. Shape into round
patties 1 1/2-inches thick. Heat Dutch oven over
medium heat. Fry patties in vegetable shortening
until well browned on both sides. Spoon off
fat. Combine soups in medium bowl. Gradually
stir in hot water. Stir in Worcestershire. Pour
over beef patties. Peel onions then cut into
1/2-inch slices. Layer over patties and gravy.
Cover pot.

Bake at 400° 25 minutes. Uncover.
Dip a tablespoon into hot gravy, then into

biscuit dough. Scoop up heaping spoonfuls, drop on top onions and gravy in 4 equal portions. Continue baking at 400° about 25 minutes until biscuits are golden brown. Makes 4 servings.

DROP BISCUIT TOPPING: Place 2 cups Ranch House Baking mix into medium bowl. Add 2/3 cup milk, stir quickly with a fork until a soft drop dough starts to form. If dough seems a little stiff, quickly stir in about 1 tablespoon milk; let stand 5 minutes.

1 tbsp butter or margarine
1 1 lb pkg beef hot dogs, cut into 1-inch chunks
2 1 lb cans cream style corn
6 tbsp milk
1/4 tsp each Worcestershire sauce and onion powder
1/8 tsp pepper
1 cups (4-oz) grated Cheddar cheese

CORNBREAD TOPPING
2 eggs
3/4 cup buttermilk
2 tbsp cooking oil
1 1/3 cups Ranch House Baking Mix
2/3 cup yellow cornmeal
1 tsp sugar
1/4 tsp each baking soda and salt

Fry hot dogs in butter in heavy iron 10 1/2-inch skillet over medium heat until lightly browned. Stir in corn, milk and seasonings. Heat mixture over low heat until hot, stirring occasionally; do not boil. Turn heat off. Sprinkle grated cheese evenly over top. Spoon cornbread topping over cheese. Carefully spread with the back of a tablespoon to make an even layer.

Bake at 400° until topping is golden brown, about 22 minutes. Let stand 10 minutes. Makes 4 servings.

CORNBREAD TOPPING: Beat eggs in medium bowl. Blend in buttermilk and oil at low speed. Place baking mix, cornmeal, sugar, baking soda and salt into small bowl. Stir with a pastry blender until well mixed. Add to buttermilk mixture. Stir with beaters to dampen, beat at low speed 1/2 minute. Scrape bowl with a rubber spatula, stir 10 turns.

BEEF PATTIES

1 egg
1 1/2 lbs lean ground beef
1/2 cup milk
1/4 cup yellow cornmeal
1/4 cup diced green peppers
2 green onions, finely minced
3 tbsp cracker crumbs
1 tbsp chili powder
1/2 tsp each seasoned salt, ground coriander and salt
1/4 tsp each garlic powder and pepper
1 tbsp each olive oil and vegetable shortening for frying

GRAVY

1 10 3/4-oz can cream of chicken soup
1 10 3/4-oz can cream of mushroom soup
1 cup milk
1 cup hot water
1 tsp each chili powder and worcestershire sauce

DROP BISCUIT TOPPING; recipe follows

BEEF PATTIES: Beat egg in medium bowl. Add remaining ingredients; stir until well mixed. Divide into 5 equal portions. Shape into round patties 3/4-inch thick. Fry in olive oil and vegetable shortening in a large skillet over medium heat until well browned on both sides. Transfer to a 13 by 9-inch baking pan. Place gravy ingredients into electric blender container. Blend at medium speed until gravy is smooth. Spoon off fat in skillet. Pour in gravy mixture. Bring to simmering over medium heat, stirring

occasionally. Pour over patties. Cover
top of pan with foil, leaving 1/2-inch free space
at long sides of pan to let steam escape.

Bake at 350° 25 minutes. Increase oven
temperature to 400°. Bake 10 minutes longer.
Remove foil. Dip a tablespoon into hot gravy,
then into biscuit dough. Scoop up heaping
spoonfuls, drop on top of patties and gravy
in 5 equal portions. Continue baking at
400° until biscuits are lightly browned,
about 20 to 25 minutes. Makes 5 servings.

DROP BISCUIT TOPPING: Combine 1 1/4 cups
Ranch House Baking Mix, 1/2 cup yellow cornmeal, 1/4 teaspoon each baking soda, baking
powder, sugar and 1/8 teaspoon salt in
medium bowl. Stir with pastry blender until
well mixed. Add 2/3 cup buttermilk, stir
quickly with a fork until a soft drop dough
forms; let stand 5 minutes.

1 1/2 lbs lean ground beef
1 10 3/4 - oz can cream of celery soup
1 10 3/4 - oz can cream of mushroom soup
2/3 cup hot water
1/4 cup milk
1 tbsp catsup
1/2 tsp each Worcestershire sauce and onion powder
1/4 tsp pepper
1/8 tsp each garlic powder and paprika
1 cup commercial sour cream

BISCUIT TOPPING
2 1/2 cups Ranch House Baking mix
2/3 cup milk

Fry ground beef in Dutch oven over medium-to-high heat until red color leaves meat, breaking up chunks as it cooks. Spoon off fat. Continue frying until lightly browned. Stir in remaining ingredients, except sour cream. Bring to simmering over medium heat, stirring occasionally. Add sour cream. Stir over low heat until mixture is hot; do not boil. Transfer to a 13 by 9-inch baking pan. Top with 8 biscuits.

Bake at 400° 22 to 25 minutes until biscuits are lightly browned. Makes 4 servings.

BISCUIT TOPPING: Place baking mix into medium bowl. Add milk, stir quickly with a fork until barely mixed. If dough seems a little stiff add about 1 to 1 1/2 tablespoons milk, stir quickly until a soft dough forms; let stand 5 minutes. With a rubber spatula remove dough to a floured surface. With floured hands round up into a ball. Lightly coat with flour, knead lightly 8 times. Pat out with floured palm of hand or roll dough about 3/4-inch thick. Cut with floured 2 1/4-inch cutter. Remove rounds to one side of floured surface. Gather up trimmings, lay on top of each other then lightly press together. Pat out dough, cut out rounds.

PINTO BEAN CASSEROLE

1 1/2 lbs lean ground beef
1 cup chopped onions
1 8-oz can tomato sauce
1 6-oz can tomato paste
1 1.25 oz package Taco seasoning, divided
1/4 tsp each seasoned salt and paprika
1/8 tsp garlic powder
1 1/4 cups hot water, divided
2 1-lb cans Pinto beans in tomato sauce

PINWHEEL BISCUIT TOPPING
2 cups Ranch House Baking mix
1/2 cup milk
1 1/4 cups meat filling, reserved

Fry ground beef in Dutch oven over medium-to-high heat until red color leaves meat, breaking up chunks as it cooks. Spoon off fat. Push meat to one side of pot. Add onions. Fry until pale golden and tender, about 10 minutes, stirring occasionally. Stir onions into meat. Continue cooking 5 minutes, stirring occasionally. Add tomato sauce, tomato paste, 1 tablespoon of the Taco seasoning, seasoned salt, paprika, garlic powder and 1/2 cup of the hot water. Cook and stir until mixture comes to boiling, then lower heat until mixture is simmering. Continue cooking and stirring until mixture is thick, about 7 minutes. Remove 1 1/4 cups to a small bowl. Cool and reserve for the pinwheel biscuits. To remaining meat mixture in pot add beans, remaining 3/4 cup hot water and remaining Taco seasoning. Stir until well mixed. Cover and bring to simmering over medium heat, stirring occasionally. Spoon into a 13 by 9-inch baking pan. Top with pinwheel biscuits.

Bake at 460° 23 to 25 minutes until biscuits are lightly browned. Makes 5 servings.

PINWHEEL BISCUITS: Place baking mix into medium bowl. Add milk, stir quickly with a fork until a slightly stiff dough forms. With a rubber spatula remove to a floured surface. Lightly coat with flour then pat dough into a 6-inch square. Roll out to a 12 by 4-inch rectangle. Smooth uneven edges with fingers. Spread reserved meat filling over surface to within 1/2-inch of edges. Roll up from 12-inch side. Moisten open edge with water; pinch firmly against side of roll to seal. Cut into 10 equal pieces.

SALISBURY CASSEROLE

BEEF PATTIES
1 egg
1 1/4 lbs lean ground beef
1/2 cup chopped onions
1/2 cup milk
1/3 cup cracker crumbs
2 tsp Worcestershire sauce
1/2 tsp seasoned salt and salt
1/4 tsp each pepper, garlic powder and nutmeg

GRAVY
1/4 cup butter or margarine
1/4 cup flour
3 cups hot milk
1 10 3/4-oz can cream of mushroom soup
1/2 tsp onion powder
1/4 tsp each pepper, seasoned salt and ground coriander
1/8 tsp thyme
12 black pitted olives

BISCUIT TOPPING
2 cups Ranch House Baking mix
1/2 cup plus 1 tbsp milk

BEEF PATTIES: Beat egg in medium bowl. Add remaining ingredients; stir until well mixed. Divide into 4 equal portions. Shape into round patties 1 1/2 - inches thick. Place on a lightly greased rimmed baking sheet.

Bake at 400° 15 minutes. Lower oven temperature to 350°; bake 20 minutes longer.

While patties are baking, prepare gravy and biscuits. GRAVY: melt butter in Dutch oven over low heat. Stir in flour with a fork until well blended. Gradually stir in hot milk. Cook and stir over medium

heat until mixture begins to thicken. Add
soup and seasonings. Cook and stir until
gravy is simmering. Add the cooked patties
and olives. Top with 4 biscuits.

Bake at 425° until biscuits are golden
brown, about 25 minutes. makes 4 servings.

BISCUIT TOPPING: Place biscuit mix into
medium bowl. Add milk, stir quickly with
a fork until barely mixed. If dough seems
a little stiff add about 1 tablespoon milk, stir
quickly until a soft dough forms; let stand
5 minutes. With a rubber spatula remove
dough to a floured surface. With floured hands
round up into a ball. Lightly coat with flour,
knead lightly 8 times. Pat out with floured
palm of hand or roll dough 3/4-inch thick.
Cut with floured 2 3/4-inch cutter. Remove 4
rounds to one side of floured surface. Gather
up trimmings, lay on top of each other then
lightly press together. Pat out dough 1/2-inch
thick. Cut with floured 2-inch cutter. Bake
extra biscuits on a small greased baking
sheet at 425° 12 minutes until golden brown.

1 recipe PRESS-IN PASTRY TOPPING (P-582)

FILLING

1/4 cup butter or margarine
5 tbsp flour
1 1/2 cups hot chicken broth; recipe follows
1 1/2 cups milk
2 1/2 cups cooked chicken chunks; recipe follows
1 cup cooked potato cubes, from a 1-lb can whole potatoes
1 cup cooked frozen peas and carrots from a 10-g pkg

Melt butter in a large skillet over low heat. Stir in flour with a fork until well blended. Remove from heat. Gradually stir in hot chicken broth. Return to medium heat. Gradually stir in milk. Cook and stir until gravy begins to thicken. Add chicken chunks, cook and stir 3 minutes. Stir in potato cubes and peas and carrots. Cover skillet and keep filling hot over very low heat, stirring occasionally.

Prepare pastry as directed. Shape into four 4-inch rounds. Bake as directed. Cool 5 minutes. Spoon chicken mixture into four 12-oz pottery baking dishes. Top with baked pastry. Makes 4 servings.

TO PREPARE CHICKEN: Place a 3 to 3 1/2 lb broiler-fryer, washed and cut up, into Dutch oven. Pour in 1 1/2 cups water. Add 1 tablespoon instant chicken bouillon granules, 1 small bay leaf, 8 peppercorns, 1/4 teaspoon seasoned salt, 1/4 teaspoon marjoram and 1/8 teaspoon poultry seasoning. Bring to boiling over high heat. Reduce heat until water is simmering. Cover. Cook chicken until tender, about 45 minutes. Let stand until cool enough to handle. Remove skin; debone chicken. Strain broth and reserve for gravy. Cut chicken into 3/4-inch chunks.

CHICKEN STEW AND DUMPLINGS

1 3 1/2 lb broiler fryer, cut into serving pieces
2 cups water
1 small peeled onion, cut into 3rds
4 tsp instant chicken bouillon granules
6 peppercorns
1 small bay leaf
1/8 tsp poultry seasoning

DUMPLINGS
1 1/2 cups Ranch House Baking Mix
1/2 cup milk

2/3 cup milk and 1/3 cup instant flour for gravy

Place washed chicken into Dutch oven. Add remaining ingredients. Bring to boiling over high heat. Lower heat until broth is simmering. Cover. Cook chicken until almost tender, about 35 minutes. Do not overcook.

DUMPLINGS: Place baking mix into small bowl. Add 1/2 cup milk, stir quickly with a fork until a soft drop dough forms; let stand 5 minutes. Dip a tablespoon into boiling broth, then into dough. Scoop up heaping spoonfuls, drop on top of chicken in 4 equal portions. Simmer dumplings over low heat, uncovered, 8 minutes. Cover, cook 8 minutes longer. Transfer chicken and dumplings to a large serving platter. Remove bay leaf, onion and peppercorns from broth with a skimmer. Combine milk and instant flour in a 1-cup measure. Gradually stir into boiling broth. Cook and stir over low heat until gravy thickens. Ladle over chicken and dumplings on platter. Makes 4 servings.

MEXICALI CHICKEN CASSEROLE

2 1/2 cups cooked chicken chunks; recipe follows
1/4 cups butter or margarine
1/4 cups flour
1 1/2 tbsp Taco seasoning, from a 1.25 oz envelope
1 1/2 cups hot chicken broth, reserved from cooked chicken
1 cup milk

BISCUIT TOPPING
1 1/4 cups Ranch House Baking mix
1/4 cups plus 1 tbsp milk
1 cup (4-oz) grated Jack cheese with Jalapeño peppers

PREPARE CHICKEN: Place a 3 to 3 1/2 lb broiler-fryer, washed and cut up, into Dutch oven. Add 1 1/2 cups water and 1 teaspoon instant chicken bouillon granules. Bring to boiling over high heat. Lower heat until broth is simmering. Cover. Cook chicken until tender, about 45 minutes. Let stand until cool enough to handle. Skin and debone chicken. Cut into 1-inch chunks. Strain and reserve broth for gravy.

Melt butter in medium skillet over low heat. Combine flour and Taco seasoning in a 1-cup measure. Stir into melted butter with a fork. Remove from heat. Gradually stir in hot chicken broth. Return to medium heat. Gradually stir in milk. Cook and stir until gravy is smooth and begins to thicken. Add chicken chunks. Cook and stir 3 minutes. Turn heat off; cover pan.

BISCUIT TOPPING: Place baking mix into small bowl. Add milk, stir quickly with a fork until barely mixed. If dough seems a little stiff add about 1/2 to 3/4 tablespoon milk, stir quickly until a soft dough forms; let stand 5 minutes. With a rubber spatula remove dough to a floured surface. With floured hands round up into a ball. Lightly coat with flour, knead lightly 8 times. Pat out with floured hand to a 4-inch square. Cut crosswise in half, then cut through center of dough lengthwise to make four 2-inch squares. Separate biscuits. Make a deep depression 3/4-inch wide in center of each biscuit with floured thumb. Spoon chicken mixture into a greased 8-inch square glass baking dish. Top with biscuits. Sprinkle 1/2 of the grated cheese over biscuit tops.

Bake at 400° 15 minutes. Sprinkle remaining grated cheese over biscuits. Bake 10 minutes longer. Makes 4 servings.

3 1/2 cups cooked chicken chunks; recipe follows
1 10 3/4-oz can cream of chicken soup
1 10 3/4-oz can cream of mushroom soup
1 cup commercial sour cream
1/4 cup milk
1/8 tsp each poultry seasoning and pepper

BISCUIT TOPPING
2 1/2 cups Ranch House Baking Mix
2/3 cup milk

PREPARE CHICKEN: Place 4 large pieces each washed chicken breasts, thighs and drumsticks in 13 by 9-inch baking pan. Add 1/4 cup water. (Do not add salt.) Cover pan tightly with foil.

Bake at 350° 1 to 1 1/2 hours until chicken is tender. Cool to lukewarm. Skin and debone chicken. Cut into 1-inch chunks. Wash baking pan.

Combine soup, sour cream, milk and seasonings in large bowl. Beat at low speed until blended. Stir in chicken chunks. Spoon into 13 by 9-inch baking pan. Cover with foil.

Bake at 400° 20 minutes or until gravy is hot. Remove foil. Top with 10 biscuits. Bake 22 to 25 minutes or until biscuits are lightly browned. Makes 5 servings.

BISCUIT TOPPING: Place baking mix into medium bowl. Add milk, stir quickly with a fork until barely mixed. If dough seems a little stiff add about 1 to 1 1/2 tablespoons milk, stir quickly until a soft dough forms; let stand 5 minutes. With a rubber spatula remove dough to a floured surface. With floured hands round up into a ball. Lightly coat with flour, Knead lightly 8 times. Pat out with floured palm of hand or roll dough about 1/2-inch thick. Cut with floured 2 1/4-inch biscuit cutter. Gather up trimmings, lay on top of each other then lightly press together. Pat out dough, cut out rounds.

SMOTHERED CHICKEN

1 3 to 3 1/2 lb broiler-fryer, cut into serving pieces
2 10 3/4-oz cans cream of chicken soup
2 cups water
1/2 cup instant flour
1/2 tsp each poultry seasoning and pepper
DROP BISCUIT TOPPING
2 cups Ranch House Baking mix
2/3 cups milk

Place washed chicken into a 12 1/2-inch oval roasting pan. Place soup, water, flour and seasonings into electric blender container. Blend at low speed until smooth. Pour over chicken.

Bake at 375°, uncovered, until chicken is almost tender, about 1 1/4 hours. Increase oven temperature to 400°. Dip a tablespoon into hot gravy, then into biscuit dough. Scoop up heaping spoonfuls, drop on top of chicken in 4 equal portions. Bake until biscuits are golden brown, about 25 minutes. Makes 4 servings.

DROP BISCUIT TOPPING: Place baking mix into medium bowl. Add milk, stir quickly with a fork until a soft drop dough starts to form. If dough seems a little stiff, quickly stir in about 1 tablespoon milk; let stand 5 minutes.

1 3 to 3 1/2 lb broiler - roaster, cut into serving pieces
1 10 3/4 - oz can cream of chicken soup
2 tbsp flour
1 envelope onion soup mix
1 cup water
1/2 tsp Worcestershire sauce
1/2 tsp pepper
1/4 tsp ground coriander
DROP BISCUIT TOPPING
1 1/2 cups Ranch House Baking mix
1/2 cup milk

Place washed chicken into a 12 1/2 - inch oval roasting pan. Combine chicken soup and flour in small bowl with a spoon. Blend in onion soup mix. Stir in remaining ingredients. Pour over chicken. Cover.

Bake at 350° 35 minutes. Stir gravy until well mixed. Continue baking until chicken is almost tender, about 20 minutes longer. Increase oven temperature to 400°. Uncover. Dip a tablespoon into hot gravy, then into biscuit dough. Scoop up heaping spoonfuls, drop on top of chicken in 4 equal portions. Bake, uncovered, until biscuits are golden brown, about 25 minutes. If gravy needs thinning, stir in enough hot water to thin to desired consistency. Makes 4 servings.

DROP BISCUIT TOPPING: Place baking mix into small bowl. Add milk, stir quickly with a fork until a soft drop dough forms; let stand 5 minutes.

SWISS CHICKEN CASSEROLE

1 3 lb broiler-fryer, cut into serving pieces
2 cups water
1 tbsp instant chicken bouillon granules
1 tbsp tomato paste
1 small bay leaf
1/2 tsp onion powder
1/4 tsp each basil leaves, poultry seasoning and thyme
1/8 tsp each tarragon leaves, nutmeg and pepper
1/2 cup milk and 1/4 cup instant flour for gravy

DROP BISCUIT TOPPING
2 cups Ranch House Baking Mix
3 tbsp grated Parmesan cheese
1/2 tsp onion powder
1/8 tsp ground coriander

Place washed chicken into Dutch oven. Add water, bouillon, tomato paste, bay leaf, onion powder and seasonings. Bring to boiling over high heat. Lower heat until broth is simmering. Cover. Cook chicken until tender, about 45 minutes. With a slotted spoon, transfer chicken to a 13 by 9-inch baking pan. Strain broth into a 4-cup measure. If broth measures less than 3 cups, add hot water to bring up to 3-cup level. Pour back into washed Dutch oven. Bring to boiling over medium heat. Combine milk and instant flour. Stir into broth. Continue cooking and stirring until gravy begins to thicken. Pour over chicken in pan. Dip a tablespoon into the hot gravy, then into biscuit dough. Scoop up heaping spoonfuls, drop on top of chicken in 4 equal portions.

Bake at 400° until biscuits are golden brown, about 25 minutes. Makes 4 servings.

DROP BISCUIT TOPPING: Place baking mix into medium bowl. Stir in grated cheese, onion powder and coriander. Add milk; stir quickly with a fork until a soft drop dough starts to form. If dough seems a little stiff, quickly stir in about 1 tablespoon milk; let stand 5 minutes.

BEEF STROGANOFF PIE

1 recipe YEAST PRESS-IN PASTRY (P-588)

FILLING

1 lb lean ground beef
3/4 cup frozen chopped onions, unthawed
1/2 cup beef gravy, from a 10 1/2-oz can
1 tbsp catsup
1/2 tsp garlic salt
1/8 tsp each pepper and paprika
salt to taste
1/2 cup commercial sour cream
1 1/2 tbsp instant flour

STROGANOFF GRAVY

1/2 cup sour cream
1/2 cup beef gravy, from a 10 1/2-oz can

PREPARE PASTRY; place on a 16-inch length of waxed paper. Pat out to a 6-inch circle. Wrap in the waxed paper; place in a small baking pan. Quick chill in freezer 30 minutes.

FILLING: Fry ground beef in Dutch oven over medium-to-high heat until red color leaves meat. Spoon off fat. Push meat to one side of pot. Add onions. Fry over low-to-medium heat until tender, about 8 minutes, stirring occasionally. Stir onions into meat. Continue cooking 5 minutes, stirring occasionally. Stir in gravy, catsup and seasonings. Simmer 5 minutes. Add salt to taste. Stir sour cream and

flour together in a 1-cup measure. Add
to meat mixture. Cook and stir over medium
heat 2 minutes. Remove from heat; cool
to lukewarm.

Place chilled pastry on a floured
surface. Lightly coat with flour. Roll
out to a 12 1/2-inch circle. Fold in half,
then place into a 9-inch glass pie pan;
unfold. Press with fingers to form a
shell. Spoon in filling. Trim pastry,
leaving a 1/4-inch overhang. Turn down pastry
to form a border around filling. Crimp
sides of pastry against pan with a fork
to anchor. Let stand in a warm place
30 minutes.

Bake at 350° 25 to 30 minutes
until filling is hot and crust is golden
brown. Cool 10 minutes. Serve with
Stroganoff Gravy. Makes 4 servings.

STROGANOFF GRAVY: Combine gravy
and sour cream in small saucepan.
Cook and stir over low heat until
mixture is hot; do not boil.

HAM AND CHEESE PIE

1 recipe YEAST PRESS-IN PASTRY (P-588)

FILLING
2 cups 1/2-inch cubes cooked ham
4-oz Swiss cheese, cut into 1/2-inch cubes
4-oz Jack cheese, cut into 1/2-inch cubes
2 eggs
1/4 cup commercial sour cream
1/4 cup cream of mushroom soup, from a 10 3/4-oz can
2 tbsp grated Parmesan cheese
1/2 tsp onion powder
1/8 tsp pepper

PREPARE PASTRY; place on a 16-inch length of waxed paper. Pat out to a 6-inch circle. Wrap in the waxed paper; place in a small baking pan. Quick chill in freezer 30 minutes. Transfer to a floured surface. Lightly coat with flour. Roll out to a 13-inch circle. Fold in half, place into a 10-inch glass pie pan; unfold. Press with fingers to form a shell. Spoon in filling. Trim pastry even with rim. Roll down edges of pastry to within 1/2-inch of filling. Crimp against sides of pan with a fork to anchor.

Bake at 325° 30 to 35 minutes or until crust is golden brown. Cool 10 minutes before cutting. Makes 6 servings.

FILLING: Place ham and cheese in large bowl. Beat eggs in small bowl. Blend in remaining ingredients at low speed. Stir into ham-cheese mixture until well mixed.

KNOCKWURST PIE

1 recipe YEAST PRESS-IN PASTRY (P-588)

FILLING
1 tbsp butter or margarine
2 cups 1/3-inch cubes Knockwurst (about 3/4 lb)
3 green onions, finely sliced
1/4 cups sour cream
1/4 cups salad dressing
2 tbsp instant flour
1 cup (4-oz) grated Swiss cheese
1/8 tsp pepper

PREPARE PASTRY; place on a 16-inch length of waxed paper. Pat out to a 6-inch circle. Wrap in the waxed paper; place in a small baking pan. Quick chill in freezer 30 minutes.

FILLING: Melt butter in small skillet over medium heat. Fry knockwurst until lightly browned, stirring occasionally. Add green onions. Cook and stir 2 minutes. Remove from heat. Tilt skillet and let fat flow to one side of pan. Soak up fat with a paper towel. Cool. Combine sour cream, salad dressing and instant flour in small bowl. Sprinkle grated cheese and pepper over knockwurst. Stir in sour cream mixture; set aside.

Place chilled pastry on a floured surface. Lightly coat with flour. Roll out to a 12 1/2-inch circle. Fold in half, then place in a 9-inch glass pie pan; unfold. Press with fingers to form a shell. Spoon in filling. Trim pastry, leaving a 1/4-inch overhang. Turn down pastry to form a border around filling. Crimp sides of pastry against pan with a fork to anchor.

Let stand in a warm place 30 minutes.

Bake at 375° 5 minutes. Lower heat to 350°. Bake 20 minutes longer or until crust is golden brown. Cool 10 minutes before cutting. Makes 4 servings.

SWISS SOUFFLE' PIE

1 recipe YEAST PRESS-IN PASTRY (P-588)

FILLING
2 egg yolks
1/4 cup evaporated milk
1 tbsp flour
1/2 tsp onion powder
1/8 tsp each salt, seasoned salt and pepper
1/3 cup sour cream
2 cups (8-oz) grated Swiss cheese
2 egg whites
1/4 tsp cream of tartar

PREPARE PASTRY; place on a 16-inch length of waxed paper. Pat out to a 6-inch circle. Wrap in the waxed paper; place in a small baking pan. Quick chill in freezer 30 minutes. Transfer to a floured surface. Lightly coat with flour. Roll out to a 12 1/2-inch circle. Fold in half, place into a 9-inch glass pie pan; unfold. Press with fingers to form a shell. Trim pastry even with rim. Partially bake shell at 350° 8 minutes. Place on cooling rack. With the back of a tablespoon, press bottom and sides of shell flat. Cool.

FILLING: Beat egg yolks, evaporated milk, flour and seasonings in medium bowl at medium speed 2 minutes. Blend in sour cream at low speed. Fold in grated cheese; set aside. Beat egg whites and cream of tartar in another medium bowl until stiff peaks form. Fold 1/3 of the cheese mixture into egg whites, then fold back into remaining cheese mixture. Pour into cooled shell.

Bake at 350° 22 minutes or until a skewer inserted 1-inch from center comes out clean. Cool 10 minutes before cutting. Makes 4 to 5 servings.

YORKSHIRE BEEF PIE

FILLING
1 lb lean ground beef
1/2 cup chopped onions
1/2 cup beef gravy, from a 10 1/2-oz can
1/4 tsp seasoned salt
1/8 tsp each Old Bay seasoning and lemon flavored salt
3/4 cup cooked cubed potatoes, from a 1-lb can whole potatoes

BATTER
4 eggs
1 cup milk
1 1/3 cups Ranch House Baking mix
1 1/2 tbsp butter for pan

FILLING: Fry ground beef in Dutch oven over medium-to-high heat until red color leaves meat, breaking up chunks as it cooks. Spoon off fat. Push meat to one side of pot. Add onions. Fry over low-to-medium heat until pale golden and tender, about 10 minutes, stirring occasionally. Stir onions into meat. Add gravy and seasonings. (Reserve remaining gravy in can.) Cook and stir 5 minutes. Stir in cubed potatoes. Turn heat off. Cover pot and let stand while preparing batter.

Preheat oven to 400°. Place butter into 11-inch metal pie pan. Heat in oven 4 minutes while preparing batter.

BATTER: Place eggs, milk and baking mix into electric blender container. Blend at medium speed 1 minute. Scrape down sides of container with a rubber spatula. Blend at medium speed 1 minute. Pour batter into hot pan. Carefully spoon meat mixture over batter to within 1 1/2-inches of edges. Spread to make an even layer. (Batter will flow into meat mixture.)

Bake at 400° 20 minutes. Lower heat to 350°. Bake 20 minutes longer. Let stand 10 minutes. Heat reserved gravy in small saucepan until simmering, thinning with a small amount of hot water if desired. Cut pie into 5 to 6 servings. Transfer to serving plates. Spoon with a small amount of gravy, dividing evenly.

ENTREE PUFF SHELLS

4 SHELLS
2 tbsp butter or margarine
½ cup hot water
¾ cups Ranch House Baking Mix
2 eggs

6 SHELLS
3 tbsp butter or margarine
¾ cups hot water
1 cup plus 2 tbsp Ranch House Baking Mix
3 eggs

8 SHELLS
¼ cups butter or margarine
1 cup hot water
1 ½ cups Ranch House Baking Mix
4 eggs

TO PREPARE 4 SHELLS: Melt butter in small saucepan over low heat. (Use a medium saucepan for 6 to 8 shells.) Add hot water. Bring to boiling over high heat, then lower heat until water is simmering. Add baking mix. Stir with a wooden spoon until mixture forms a smooth ball, about 1 minute. Turn heat off; continue stirring 1 minute. Remove saucepan from heat; cool 1 minute. Add 1 egg. (Add 2 eggs for 6 to 8 shells.) Beat with spoon until smooth. Add remaining egg. Beat with electric mixer at medium speed 1 minute. Scrape sides and bottom of pan with a rubber spatula. Beat at medium speed 1 minute. Scrape pan; let stand 10 minutes. Drop dough onto a lightly greased baking sheet in 4 equal portions, spacing about 3 ½ inches apart. With a dinner knife, smooth dough upward into a rounded mound.

Bake at 400° 15 minutes. Lower temperature to 300°. Bake 30 to 35 minutes longer until shells are deep golden in color. Remove to cooling rack with a pancake turner. Let stand until cool enough to handle, about 5 to 8 minutes. With the tip of a small sharp knife, cut into shell near the top, then cut all around to make a 3-inch removable top. Remove any soft portions of dough remaining inside shell.

TO SERVE: Fill with hot filling of your choice, using about 1/2 cup for each puff. Replace top. Serve immediately.

NOTE: Shells may be baked in advance, then frozen up to 3 months. When ready to serve, thaw shells. Place on a baking sheet. Heat in oven at 350°, uncovered, 8 to 10 minutes. Fill as directed above.

BEEF STROGANOFF PUFFS

5 baked ENTREE PUFF SHELLS (P-482)
FILLING
1 tbsp vegetable shortening
1 lb lean ground beef
1 cup frozen chopped onions, unthawed
1 10 3/4-oz can cream of mushroom soup
1/4 cup hot water
1 4-oz can sliced mushrooms, drained
1/4 tsp each pepper, paprika and garlic powder
1 cup commercial sour cream

Heat Dutch oven or large skillet over medium-to-high heat. Melt shortening; add ground beef. Fry until red color leaves meat. Stir occasionally to break up chunks of meat. Spoon off all but 1 tablespoon fat. Push meat to one side of pan. Add onions. Cook over medium heat until tender, stirring occasionally. Stir onions into meat. Continue cooking until meat is lightly browned. Add mushroom soup, hot water, mushrooms and seasoning. Cook and stir over medium heat 5 minutes. Add sour cream, cook and stir until mixture is hot, about 3 minutes. Fill each hot puff shell with 1/2 cup filling; replace tops. Serve immediately. Makes 5 servings.

CHICKEN PUFFS

6 baked ENTREE PUFF SHELLS (P-482)

FILLING
1/4 cup butter or margarine
1 cup chopped frozen onions, unthawed
3 tbsp flour
1 1/2 cups milk
2 tsp instant chicken bouillon granules
1/8 tsp pepper
2 cups 3/8-inch cubes cooked chicken
2 hard-cooked eggs, coarsely chopped

Melt butter in a large skillet over low to medium heat. Add onions. Increase heat to medium. Saute' onions until tender, 5 to 8 minutes. Add flour, stir with fork until well blended. Remove from heat. Gradually stir in milk. Return to low heat. Cook and stir until smooth and thick. Stir in bouillon and pepper, then add chicken and chopped eggs. Cook 5 minutes, stirring occasionally. Fill each hot puff shell with 1/2 cup filling; replace top. Serve immediately. Makes 6 servings.

HOT DOG PUFFS

6 baked ENTREE PUFF SHELLS (P-482)

FILLING
3 tbsp butter or margarine, divided
8 hot dogs, sliced into 1/4-inch rings
1 cup chopped frozen onions, unthawed
3 tbsp flour
1 1/2 cups milk
salt and pepper to taste
4-oz Jack cheese with jalapeno peppers, cut
   into 3/8-inch cubes

Melt 1 tablespoon of the butter in a large skillet over low to medium heat. Add hot dogs; fry until lightly browned. Remove to a bowl with a slotted spoon. Add remaining 2 tablespoons butter to skillet. When melted, add onions. Saute' over medium heat until tender, 5 to 8 minutes, stirring occasionally. Add flour, stir with fork until well blended. Remove from heat. Gradually stir in milk. Return to low heat. Cook and stir until thick and smooth. Add hot dogs. Cook 5 minutes, stirring occasionally. Add salt and pepper to taste. Add Jack cheese. Cook and stir 1 to 2 minutes until cheese softens; do not melt cheese. Fill each hot puff shell with 1/2 cup filling; replace top. Serve immediately. Makes 6 servings.

SHRIMP PUFFS

6 baked ENTREE PUFF SHELLS (P-482)

FILLING
1/4 cup butter or margarine
3 tbsp flour
1 1/2 cups milk
1 1/2 tsp onion powder
1/4 tsp garlic powder
1/8 tsp pepper
2 1/2 cups small cooked shrimp
salt to taste

Melt butter in a large skillet over low-to-medium heat. Add flour, stir with fork until well blended. Remove from heat. Gradually stir in milk. Return to low heat. Cook and stir until thick and smooth. Stir in seasonings, then add shrimp. Cook 5 minutes, stirring occasionally. Add salt to taste. Fill each hot puff shell with 1/2 cup filling; replace tops. Serve immediately. Makes 6 servings.

6 baked ENTREE PUFF SHELLS (P-482)
FILLING
3 tbsp butter or margarine, divided
2 cups 3/8-inch cubes cooked ham
1 cup chopped frozen onions, unthawed
1/2 cup diced frozen green peppers, unthawed
3 tbsp flour
1 1/2 cups hot water
1 tsp instant beef bouillon granules
1/8 tsp pepper
4-oz Swiss cheese, cut into 3/8-inch cubes

Melt 1 tablespoon of the butter in a large skillet over low-to-medium heat. Add ham; fry until lightly browned, stirring occasionally. Transfer to a bowl with a slotted spoon. Add remaining 2 tablespoons butter to skillet. When melted add onions and green peppers. Sauté over medium heat until tender, about 8 minutes, stirring occasionally. Stir in flour with a fork until well blended. Remove from heat. Gradually stir in hot water. Return to low heat. Cook and stir until thick and smooth. Stir in bouillon and pepper, then add ham. Cook 5 minutes, stirring occasionally. Add Swiss cheese. Cook and stir 1 to 2 minutes until cheese softens; do not melt cheese. Fill each hot puff shell with 1/2 cup filling; replace top. Serve immediately. Makes 6 servings.

CRUSTLESS BACON AND CORN QUICHE

1 cups drained canned corn
1/2 cup frozen chopped onions, unthawed
6 slices crisply fried bacon, crumbled
3 eggs
1 1/4 cups milk
1/2 cup Ranch House Baking mix
1/8 tsp each salt and pepper

Grease a 9-inch glass pie pan. Spoon in corn. Sprinkle with onions and bacon; set aside.

Place eggs, milk, baking mix, salt and pepper into electric blender container. Blend at medium speed 1 minute. Scrape down sides of container with a rubber spatula. Blend at medium speed 1/2 minute. Pour over corn mixture.

Bake at 375° 25 to 30 minutes or until a skewer inserted 1-inch from center comes out clean. Let stand 10 minutes before cutting. makes 4 to 5 servings.

1 1/2 tbsp butter or margarine
3/4 cup frozen chopped onions, unthawed
1 cup chopped leftover roast beef
1 tbsp catsup
1 tsp Worcestershire sauce
1/4 tsp pepper
1 1/2 cups (6-oz) grated Cheddar cheese, divided
3 eggs
1 1/2 cups milk
1/2 cup Ranch House Baking mix
1/8 tsp salt

Melt butter in small skillet over low to medium heat. Add onions. Cook and stir until tender, about 8 minutes, stirring occasionally. Stir in chopped meat, catsup, Worcestershire and pepper. Cook and stir 1 minute. Spoon into a greased 9-inch glass pie pan. Sprinkle with 1 cup grated cheese; set aside.

Place eggs, milk, baking mix and salt into electric blender container. Blend at medium speed 1 minute. Scrape down sides of container with a rubber spatula. Blend at medium speed 1/2 minute. Pour over beef-cheese mixture. Sprinkle with remaining 1/2 cup cheese.

Bake at 375° 25 to 30 minutes or until a skewer inserted 1-inch from center comes out clean. Let stand 10 minutes before cutting. Makes 4 to 5 servings.

CRUSTLESS GREEN CHILIES QUICHE

1 4-oz can whole green chilies
1 cups (4-oz) grated jack cheese with jalapeño peppers
3 eggs
1 1/2 cups milk
1/2 cup Ranch House Baking mix
1/8 tsp salt

Drain chilies; remove seeds. Layer into bottom of a greased 9-inch glass pie pan. Sprinkle with grated cheese; set aside.

Place eggs, milk, baking mix and salt into electric blender container. Blend at medium speed 1 minute. Scrape down sides of container with a rubber spatula. Blend at medium speed 1/2 minute. Pour over chilies and cheese.

Bake at 375° 25 to 30 minutes or until a skewer inserted 1-inch from center comes out clean. Let stand 10 minutes before cutting. Makes 4 to 5 servings.

CRUSTLESS HAM QUICHE

1 cup chopped cooked ham
1 cup (4-oz) grated Swiss cheese
3 eggs
1 1/4 cups milk
1/2 cup Ranch House Baking mix
1/2 tsp onion powder
1/8 tsp pepper

Grease a 9-inch glass pie pan. Spoon in ham. Lightly press to make an even layer. Top with grated cheese; set aside.

Place eggs, milk, baking mix, onion powder and pepper into electric blender container. Blend at medium speed 1 minute. Scrape down sides of container with a rubber spatula. Blend at medium speed 1/2 minute. Pour over ham-cheese mixture.

Bake at 375° 25 to 30 minutes or until a skewer inserted 1-inch from center comes out clean. Let stand 10 minutes before cutting. Makes 4 to 5 servings.

CRUSTLESS MEXICAN QUICHE

½ lb lean ground beef
½ cup chopped onions
2 tbsp Taco seasoning, from a 1.25 oz package
½ cup hot water
1 cup (4-oz) grated Jack cheese with jalapeño peppers
3 eggs
1 ½ cups milk (⅛ tsp red pepper sauce, optional
¼ cup each Ranch House Baking mix and yellow cornmeal
⅛ tsp salt
½ cup (2-oz) grated Cheddar cheese

Fry ground beef in small skillet over medium-to-high heat until red color leaves meat. Spoon off fat. Push meat to one side of pan. Add onions. Cook over low-to-medium heat until tender, about 10 minutes, stirring occasionally. Stir onions into meat. Continue cooking 5 minutes, stirring occasionally. Stir in Taco seasoning and hot water. Cook and stir until mixture thickens, about 3 minutes. Spoon into a greased 10-inch glass pie pan. Cool 30 minutes. Sprinkle with grated Jack cheese; set aside.

Place eggs, milk, baking mix, cornmeal and salt into electric blender container. Blend at medium speed 1 minute. Scrape down sides of container with a rubber spatula. Blend at medium speed ½ minute. Pour over meat-cheese mixture. Sprinkle with grated Cheddar cheese.

Bake at 375° 30 minutes or until a skewer inserted 1-inch from center comes out clean. Let stand 10 minutes before cutting. Makes 5 to 6 servings.

CRUSTLESS SHRIMP QUICHE

1 1/2 tbsp butter or margarine
1 1/4 cups coarsely chopped cooked shrimp
3 green onions, finely sliced
1/8 tsp each paprika, lemon flavored salt,
    garlic salt and Old Bay seasoning
3 eggs
1 1/4 cups milk
1/2 cups Ranch House Baking mix

melt butter in small skillet over medium heat. Add shrimp, green onions and seasonings. Cook and stir 5 minutes. Spoon into a greased 9-inch glass pie pan. Cool 5 minutes.

Place eggs, milk and baking mix into electric blender container. Blend at medium speed 1 minute. Scrape down sides of container with a rubber spatula. Blend at medium speed 1/2 minute. Pour over shrimp mixture.

Bake at 375° 25 to 30 minutes or until a skewer inserted 1-inch from center comes out clean. Let stand 10 minutes before cutting. makes 4 to 5 servings.

CRUSTLESS TURKEY QUICHE

1 cup coarsely chopped leftover roast turkey,
   lightly pkd in cup
1/2 cup frozen onions, unthawed
3 eggs
1 1/4 cups milk
1/2 cup Ranch House Baking mix
1/2 tsp Old Bay seasoning
1/4 tsp seasoned salt
1 cup (4-oz) grated Swiss cheese

Grease a 9-inch glass pie pan. Spoon
in turkey; press to make an even layer. Sprinkle
with onion; set aside.

Place eggs, milk, baking mix and seasonings
into electric blender container. Blend at medium
speed 1 minute. Scrape down sides of container
with a rubber spatula. Blend at medium
speed 1/2 minute. Pour over turkey. Sprinkle
with grated cheese.

Bake at 375° 25 to 30 minutes or until
a skewer inserted 1-inch from center comes
out clean. Let stand 10 minutes before
cutting. Makes 4 to 5 servings.

BACON AND CHEESE BUNS

4 SANDWICH BUNS for hamburgers (P-149)
½ cups bottled chili sauce
1 cups (4-oz) grated Cheddar cheese
1 cups (4-oz) grated jack cheese
6 slices crisp cooked bacon, cut in half

Cut buns in half horizontally. Spread each cut side with 1 tablespoon chili sauce. Place ¼ of the grated cheddar cheese on each bun bottom. Place 3 strips bacon over cheese. Top with ¼ of the grated jack cheese. Place bun tops over cheese. Wrap in foil. Place package on a baking sheet.

Heat in oven 350° 22 minutes. Makes 4 servings.

BARBEQUED BEEF BUNS

4 SANDWICH BUNS for hamburgers (P-149)

FILLING
3/4 lb lean ground beef
1/2 large onion, chopped
1/2 medium green pepper, diced
1/2 cup bottled smoke flavored barbeque sauce
1/2 cup tomato sauce
1 tbsp Prime choice sauce
1/2 tsp seasoned salt
1/4 tsp ground coriander
3 drops Tobasco sauce

FILLING: Heat Dutch oven over medium-to-high heat. Add ground beef. Fry until red color leaves meat; stir occasionally to break up large chunks. Spoon off all but 1 tablespoon fat. Push meat to one side of pan. Add onions and green peppers. Sauté over low-to-medium heat until tender, about 8 minutes, then stir into meat. Add remaining filling ingredients. Bring to boiling over high heat. Lower heat until sauce is simmering. Cook, uncovered, until thick, about 30 minutes, stirring frequently.

Cut buns in half horizontally. Wrap in foil. Place package on a baking sheet. Heat in oven 350° 15 minutes. Spoon filling over bottom half of buns. Top with upper half of buns. makes 4 servings.

BLT AND GUACAMOLE BUNS

4 SANDWICH BUNS for hamburgers (P-149)
FILLING
1/2 recipe (1 cup) GUACAMOLE (P-430)
lettuce
sliced tomatoes
mayonnaise
6 slices crisp cooked bacon, cut in half

Cut buns in half horizontally. Wrap in foil. Place package on baking sheet. Heat in oven at 325° 15 minutes.

ASSEMBLE BUNS: Spread 1/4 cup Guacamole over bottom half of each warm bun. Top with lettuce. Spread one side of thinly sliced tomatoes with mayonnaise, using 2 to 3 slices for each bun. Place over lettuce, mayonnaise side down. Place 3 strips warm bacon over tomatoes. Top with lettuce. Spread cut side of bun top with mayonnaise. Place over lettuce. Makes 4 servings.

CHICKEN SALAD BUNS

6 SANDWICH BUNS for hamburgers (P-149)

FILLING
1 1/2 cups finely chopped cooked chicken
1/2 cup finely chopped celery
1 finely chopped green onion
6 tbsp mayonnaise
2 tbsp salad dressing
1 tsp lemon juice
salt and pepper to taste
lettuce
mayonnaise or salad dressing

Cut buns in half horizontally. Wrap in foil. Place package on a baking sheet. Heat in oven 325° 15 minutes.

FILLING: Place chicken, celery and green onion in medium bowl. Combine mayonnaise, salad dressing and lemon juice in small bowl. Stir into chicken mixture until well blended. Add salt and pepper to taste. Spread filling over bottom half of each warm bun, dividing evenly. Top with lettuce. Spread mayonnaise or salad dressing over cut side of bun tops. Place over lettuce. makes 6 servings.

CORN BEEF BUNS

4 SANDWICH BUNS for hamburgers (P-149)
FILLING
1 cup chopped cooked corn beef
3/4 cup (3-oz) grated Swiss cheese
3 tbsp. salad dressing
2 tbsp mayonnaise
1 tsp prepared mustard
1/2 tsp Worcestershire sauce
1/4 tsp each pepper and onion powder

FILLING: Combine ingredients in medium bowl until well mixed. Cut buns in half horizontally. Spread bottom half with 1/3 cup filling. Top with upper bun half. Wrap in foil. Place package on a baking sheet.

Heat in oven 350° 22 minutes. Makes 4 servings.

CRAB BOATS

2 SANDWICH BUNS for steaks (P-149)

FILLING
1/3 cup mayonnaise
1 tbsp salad dressing
1 tsp Worcestershire sauce
1/2 tsp prepared mustard
1/4 tsp onion powder
1/8 tsp pepper
1 cup shredded cooked crabmeat
3/4 cup (3-oz) grated jack, muenster or Provolone cheese

Combine mayonnaise, salad dressing, worcestershire, mustard, onion powder and pepper in medium bowl. Fold in crab and cheese. Cut buns in half lengthwise. Spoon with filling, dividing evenly. Spread to cover buns, slightly mounding in center lengthwise. Place on baking sheet.

Bake at 375° 10 to 12 minutes. Makes 4 servings.

4 SANDWICH BUNS for hamburgers (P-149)

FILLING

1/4 cups mayonnaise
1 1/2 tbsp sour cream
1 1/2 tbsp bottled chili sauce
1/2 tbsp chopped block olives
1 tsp sweet pickle relish
1/8 tsp pepper
1 cup shredded cooked crabmeat
lettuce
mayonnaise or salad dressing

Cut buns in half horizontally.
Wrap in foil. Place package on a baking
sheet. Heat in oven 325° 15 minutes.

FILLING: Combine mayonnaise,
sour cream, chili sauce, olives, pickle
relish and pepper in small bowl. Fold
in crabmeat. Spread 1/4 cup filling
over bottom half of each warm bun.
Top with lettuce. Spread mayonnaise
or salad dressing over cut side of bun
tops. Place over lettuce. Makes 4
servings.

HAM BUNS

6 SANDWICH BUNS for hamburgers (P-149)

FILLING
1 tbsp butter or margarine
2 green onions, finely chopped
1 1/2 cups chopped cooked ham, lightly pkd in cup
1/4 cup sour cream
2 tbsp salad dressing
1 egg yolk
1 tsp prepared mustard
1/4 tsp pepper

FILLING: melt butter in a small skillet over low-to-medium heat. Add green onions. Sauté until tender, about 5 minutes, stirring occasionally. Add ham, cook and stir 5 minutes. Let stand on burner with heat off. Combine sour cream, salad dressing, egg yolk, mustard and pepper in a small custard cup with a fork. Stir into ham mixture. Cook and stir over medium heat 3 minutes. Remove from heat. Cut buns in half horizontally. Spread bottom half with filling, dividing evenly. Top with upper bun half. Wrap in foil. Place package on a baking sheet.

Heat in oven 350° 22 minutes.
makes 6 servings.

HAM AND CHEESE BOATS

504

2 SANDWICH BUNS for steaks (P-149)

FILLING
1 3-oz pkg cream cheese, softened
2 tbsp evaporated milk
4 tsp salad dressing
2 tsp Horseradish sauce
2 tsp prepared mustard
1 cup minced cooked ham
1 cup (4-oz) grated Swiss cheese

    In medium bowl beat together cream cheese and evaporated milk with a spoon until smooth. Blend in salad dressing, Horseradish sauce and mustard. Fold in ham and cheese. Cut buns in half lengthwise. Spoon with filling, dividing evenly. Spread to cover buns, slightly mounding in center lengthwise. Place on baking sheet.

    Bake at 375° 10 to 12 minutes. Makes 4 servings.

HAM AND CHEESE BUNS

4 SANDWICH BUNS for hamburgers (P-149)

FILLING

1/4 cup mayonnaise
2 tbsp sandwich spread
1/2 tbsp prepared mustard
1/8 tsp onion powder
1/16 tsp pepper
8 slices Swiss cheese
4 slices cooked sandwich ham

Combine mayonnaise, sandwich spread, mustard, onion powder and pepper in small bowl. Cut buns in half horizontally. Spread cut sides with mayonnaise mixture. Place 1 slice cheese on bottom half of buns. Top with a slice of ham, then another slice of cheese. Place bun tops over cheese. Wrap in foil. Place package on a baking sheet.

Heat in oven 350° 22 minutes. Makes 4 servings.

2 SANDWICH BUNS for steaks (P-149)

FILLING

1/4 cup mayonnaise
3 tbsp evaporated milk
1/4 tsp dried basil leaves, crumbled
1/8 tsp dried oregano leaves, crumbled
1/8 tsp garlic salt
1 green onion, finely chopped
1 cup slivered Italian salami
1 cup (4-oz) grated mozzarella cheese

Combine mayonnaise and evaporated milk in medium bowl. Blend in basil, oregano, garlic salt and green onion. Fold in salami and cheese. Cut buns in half lengthwise. Spoon with filling, dividing evenly. Spread to cover buns, slightly mounding in center lengthwise. Place on baking sheet.

Bake at 375° 10 to 12 minutes. Makes 4 servings.

MEXE-DOG BUNS

4 SANDWICH BUNS for steaks (P-149)
FILLING
6 hot dogs, cut into 1/4-inch cubes
6-oz jack cheese with jalapeña peppers,
   cut into 1/4-inch cubes
2 green onions, finely chopped
1/4 cup mayonnaise
1/4 cup bottled chili sauce
2 tsp each taco sauce and hot dog relish
3 drops Tobasco sauce

FILLING: Place hot dogs, cheese and
green onions in medium bowl. Combine
mayonnaise, chili sauce, taco sauce, relish
and Tobasco in a 1-cup measure. Stir
into hot dog mixture until well blended.
Cut buns in half lengthwise. Spread
filling over bottom half, dividing evenly.
Top with upper bun half. Wrap in
foil. Place package on a baking sheet.

Heat in oven 350° 22 minutes.
Makes 4 servings.

SHRIMP BOATS

2 SANDWICH BUNS for steaks (P-149)

FILLING

1 3-oz pkg cream cheese, softened
1/4 cup salad dressing
2 Tbsp milk
1 tbsp grated onion
1/2 tsp Worcestershire sauce
1/8 tsp each garlic powder and pepper
1 1/2 cups chopped cooked shrimp

Beat cream cheese, salad dressing and milk in medium bowl at medium speed until smooth. Stir in grated onion, worcestershire, garlic powder and pepper. Fold in shrimp. Cut buns in half lengthwise. Spoon with filling, dividing evenly. Spread to cover buns, slightly mounding in center lengthwise. Place on baking sheet.

Bake at 375° 10 to 12 minutes. Makes 4 servings.

3 SANDWICH BUNS for steaks (P-149)

FILLING
1 12 1/2-oz can chunk light tuna in water, drained
2 green onions, finely chopped
1 cup (4-oz) grated Jack cheese
1/8 tsp pepper
mayonnaise

Place drained tuna in medium bowl.
Break up chunks with a fork. Stir in green
onions, grated cheese and pepper. Add mayonnaise
to moisten mixture. Cut buns in half lengthwise.
Spoon with filling, dividing evenly. Spread
to cover bun, slightly mounding in center lengthwise. Place on baking sheet.

Bake at 375° 10 to 12 minutes. Makes
6 servings.

1 recipe 4 serving size HOT BREAD SQUARES (P-118)

FILLING
1 7-oz can solid white tuna, drained
1 hard-cooked egg, mashed
3 tbsp sandwich spread
2 tbsp mayonnaise
2 tbsp chopped black olives
1/8 tsp each pepper and onion powder

Prepare and bake bread as directed. Place on cooling rack. Let stand in pan 1 1/2 hours. While bread is cooling, prepare filling.

FILLING: Place tuna into small bowl; flake with fingers. Add remaining ingredients. Stir with a fork until well mixed. Add more sandwich spread or mayonnaise if desired.

Cut bread into 4 equal portions. Remove from pan. Cut a pocket in each square: Starting at the soft crustless corner, cut diagonally down into soft part of bread with a sharp knife, leaving the sides with crusts intact. Fill each pocket with 1/4 of the filling, easing down into pocket with the tip of a dinner knife. Place sandwiches in center of a 24-inch length of foil; wrap. Place package on a baking sheet.

Heat in oven 350° 15 minutes. Makes 4 servings.

MEXICAN POCKET SANDWICHES

1 recipe 4 serving size HOT BREAD SQUARES (P-118)
FILLING
1 tsp olive oil
1/2 lb lean ground beef
1/2 cup frozen chopped onions, unthawed
1 4-oz can green chilies, deseeded, chopped
2 tbsp chopped black olives
1/2 tsp each chili powder and garlic salt
1/4 tsp each ground coriander and cumin powder
6 tbsp sour cream
1/2 cup (2-oz) grated Jack cheese.

Prepare and bake bread as directed. Place on cooling rack. Let stand in pan 1 1/2 hours. While bread is cooling, prepare filling.

FILLING: Heat small skillet over medium-to-high heat. Add olive oil and ground beef. Fry until red color leaves meat, breaking up chunks with a spoon as it cooks. Sponge off fat with a paper towel. Push meat to one side of pan. Add onions. Sauté over low-to-medium heat until tender, about 8 minutes. Stir onions into meat. Add chilies, olives and seasonings. Cook 5 minutes, stirring occasionally. Add sour cream. Cook and stir 2 minutes. Remove from heat; cool 5 minutes. Stir in grated cheese. Let stand 15 minutes.

Cut bread into 4 equal portions. Remove from pan. Cut a pocket in each square: Starting at the soft crustless corner, cut diagonally down into soft part of bread with a sharp knife, leaving the sides with crusts intact. Fill each pocket with 1/4 of the filling, easing down into pocket with the tip of a dinner knife. Place sandwiches in center of a 24-inch length of foil; wrap. Place package on a baking sheet.

Heat in oven 350° 16 minutes. Makes 4 servings.

BAVARIAN STEW AND DUMPLINGS

1 tbsp vegetable shortening
1 tbsp butter
2 lbs beef for stew, cut into 1 to 1½-inch chunks
1 large onion, diced
2 cloves garlic, cut in half
4 cups hot water
1 tbsp instant beef bouillon granules
1 tsp caraway seeds
1 tsp paprika
½ tsp ground coriander
¼ tsp pepper
salt to taste
⅓ cup wine vinegar
½ cup gingersnap crumbs

DUMPLINGS
1 ½ cups Ranch House Baking mix
½ cup milk

Fry meat in shortening and butter in Dutch
oven over medium-to-high heat until well
browned. Push meat to one side of pot. Add
onions and garlic. Sauté over low-to-medium
heat until pale golden and tender, about 10 minutes,
stirring occasionally. Stir onions into meat.
Add remaining ingredients, except vinegar and
gingersnaps. Bring to boiling over high heat.
Lower heat until stew is simmering. Cover.
Cook until meat is tender, about 2½ hours.
Dip a tablespoon into boiling stew, then into
dumpling dough. Scoop up heaping spoonfuls,
drop on top of stew in 4 equal portions.
Cook over low heat, uncovered, 8 minutes.
Cover, cook 8 minutes longer. While dumplings

are cooking, place wine vinegar into small saucepan. Heat until lukewarm over low heat. Remove from heat. Stir in gingersnap crumbs. Transfer dumplings to serving plate. Stir ginger- snap mixture into simmering stew. Cook and stir until thickened and smooth. If a thicker gravy is desired, combine a small amount of instant flour with cold water. Stir into stew. Makes 4 servings.

DUMPLINGS: Place baking mix into small bowl. Add milk, stir quickly with a fork until a soft drop dough forms; let stand 5 minutes.

1 tbsp vegetable shortening
1 tbsp butter
2 lbs veal for stew, cut into 1 to 1 1/2-inch chunks (see note)
1 large onion, diced
1 10 3/4-oz can tomato soup
1 8-oz can tomato sauce
1 tbsp Prime choice sauce
1 tsp Worcestershire sauce
1/2 tsp each seasoned salt, garlic powder, paprika
   and ground coriander
1 small bay leaf
hot water

DUMPLINGS
1 1/2 cups Ranch House Baking Mix
1/2 cup milk

Fry meat in shortening and butter in Dutch
oven over medium-to-high heat until well browned.
Push meat to one side of pot. Add onions. Sauté
over low-to-medium heat until pale golden and
tender, about 10 minutes, stirring occasionally.
Stir onions into meat. Add soup, tomato sauce,
Prime choice and Worcestershire sauce, seasonings and
bay leaf. Stir until well blended. Add hot water
to cover 1/2-inch above top of meat. Stir well.
Bring to boiling. Turn heat off. Cover pot, then
transfer to oven preheated at 300°. Bake until
almost tender, about 2 hours. Transfer to stove
top. Bring to boiling over medium heat. Dip
a tablespoon into stew then into dumpling dough.
Scoop up heaping spoonfuls, drop on top
of stew in 4 equal portions. Cook over
low heat, uncovered, 8 minutes. Cover, cook

8 minutes longer. Makes 4 servings.

DUMPLINGS: Place baking mix into small bowl. Add milk, stir quickly with a fork until a soft drop dough forms; let stand 5 minutes.

NOTE: Beef for stew may be substituted for the Veal. Increase baking time about 1 hour, or until meat is almost tender. Add more hot water if needed, just before dropping in dumpling dough.

2 lbs beef for stew, cut into 1 to 1 1/2-inch chunks
1 cup hot water
2/3 cups burgundy wine
1 medium onion, peeled and cut into chunks
2 peeled garlic cloves
1 10 3/4-oz can cream of mushroom soup
1 10 1/2-oz can onion soup
2 tsp Worcestershire sauce
1/4 tsp each pepper, paprika and ground coriander
DROP BISCUIT TOPPING
2 cups Ranch House Baking mix
2/3 cup milk

Place meat into Dutch oven. Place hot water, wine, onion and garlic into electric blender container. Blend at medium speed until onion and garlic is liquified. Add soup and seasonings. Blend at low speed until smooth. Pour over beef. Cover.

Bake at 250° until almost tender, about 5 hours. Increase oven temperature to 400°. Bake 15 minutes longer. Uncover. Dip a tablespoon into hot stew, then into biscuit dough. Scoop up heaping spoonfuls, drop on top of stew in 4 equal portions. Bake until biscuits are golden brown, about 22 to 25 minutes. Makes 4 servings.

DROP BISCUIT TOPPING: Place baking mix into medium bowl. Add milk, stir quickly with a fork until a soft drop dough starts to form. If dough seems a little stiff, quickly stir in about 1 tablespoon milk; let stand 5 minutes.

SAUCE
1 Tbsp olive oil
1 Tbsp butter
1 large onion, diced
1 clove garlic
3 1/2 cups tomato juice
1 8-oz can tomato sauce
1 Tbsp chili powder

MEAT BALLS
1 egg
1 1/2 lbs lean ground beef
1/2 cups milk
1/2 cup diced onion
1/4 cup yellow cornmeal
1 1/2 tsp chili powder
1 tsp lemon and herb seasoned salt
1/2 tsp cumin powder
1/4 tsp each salt, pepper and garlic powder
CORNMEAL DUMPLINGS; recipe follows

SAUCE: Heat Dutch oven over medium heat. Add olive oil and butter; stir in onion and garlic. Sauté until pale golden and tender. Add tomato juice, tomato sauce and chili powder. Bring to boiling, cover, then lower heat until mixture is simmering.

MEATBALLS: Beat egg in medium bowl. Add remaining ingredients; stir until well mixed. Shape into 10 meatballs. Drop into simmering sauce. Cover, cook 25 minutes. Dip a tablespoon into hot sauce, then into dumpling dough. Scoop up heaping spoonfuls, drop on top of meatballs in 5 equal portions. Cook dumplings, uncovered, 8 minutes. Cover, cook 8 minutes longer. Makes 5 servings.

CORNMEAL DUMPLINGS: Place 1 1/2 cups Ranch House Baking mix, 1/4 cup yellow cornmeal, 1/4 teaspoon baking powder, 1/4 teaspoon sugar and 1/8 teaspoon baking soda into a small bowl. Stir with a pastry blender until well mixed. Add 1/2 cup plus 1 tablespoon milk, stir quickly with a fork until a soft drop dough forms; let stand 5 minutes.

Muffins are super easy to make when prepared with Ranch House Baking mix. These tender muffins have a fine texture, and taste consistently good. Just be careful not to overmix, which causes heaviness and a tough texture. Spoon batter into well greased muffin-pan cups, filling about 2/3 full. If batter does not fill all of the cups, pour about 1/4-inch water into empty ones to prevent smoking. When muffins are done let stand 1 minute, then run a small spatula or sharp knife around edges of cups. Remove to a heated serving plate. If muffins are done before ready to serve, place partially on side in the cups to prevent steaming.

If your regular muffin fare is just a batch of plain ones, do try the fancier types. They will dress up a simple meal. Start with Sugar 'N Spice muffins, sure to be a breakfast pleaser. Or the Streusel muffins, layered and topped with a cinnamon laced mixture. The Orange-Frost muffins and Lemon muffins sparkle with a tangy flavor. There are other good recipes to choose from.

Store leftover muffins in refrigerator

2 or 3 days, or wrap well in plastic wrap and freeze 2 months. To reheat muffins, thaw first if frozen. Place a double thickness of folded paper towels in center of a length of foil large enough to wrap muffins. Lay a double thickness of waxed paper over paper towels. Place muffins on waxed paper, then wrap in the foil, leaving 1/2-inch free space at top to let steam escape. Place package in baking pan. Heat in oven 325° 15 to 18 minutes or until hot.

APPLESAUCE MUFFINS

2 eggs
1 cup thick unsweetened applesauce
2/3 cup sugar
1 tsp cinnamon
1/8 tsp each nutmeg and baking soda
2 tbsp cooking oil
2 1/2 cups Ranch House Baking mix

Beat eggs in medium bowl. Blend in Applesauce, sugar, spices, baking soda and oil.
Add baking mix. Stir quickly with a spoon
until mixed, but still a little lumpy. Scrape
bowl with a rubber spatula. Spoon batter
into greased 2 3/4-inch muffin-pan cups,
filling 3/4 full.

Bake at 400° 17 minutes or until center
tests done. Makes 10 muffins.

BASIC MUFFINS

2 1/4 cups Ranch House Baking mix
2 1/2 tbsp sugar
2 tbsp butter, softened
1 egg
3/4 cup milk

Place baking mix and sugar into medium bowl. Cut in butter with a pastry blender until mixture is consistency of cornmeal. Beat egg in small bowl. Blend in milk, then add to baking mix. Stir quickly with a spoon until mixed, but still a little lumpy. Scrape bowl with a rubber spatula. Spoon batter into greased 2 3/4-inch muffin-pan cups, filling 2/3 full.

Bake at 400° 15 minutes or until center tests done. Makes 10 muffins.

BLUEBERRY MUFFINS

2 1/4 cups Ranch House Baking Mix

1/3 cup sugar

1/8 tsp nutmeg

2 tbsp butter, softened

1 egg

3/4 cup milk

3/4 cup washed, well drained, fresh blueberries
   or 3/4 cup unsweetened frozen blueberries, unthawed

Place baking mix, sugar and nutmeg into medium bowl. Cut in butter with a pastry blender until mixture is consistency of cornmeal. Beat egg in small bowl. Blend in milk, then add to baking mix. Stir quickly with a spoon until mixed, but still a little lumpy. Add blueberries. Scrape bowl with a rubber spatula, stir a few turns to distribute blueberries. Spoon batter into greased 2 3/4-inch muffin-pan cups, filling 2/3 full.

Bake at 400° 15 minutes or until center tests done. Makes 11 to 12 muffins.

BRAN MUFFINS

1 egg
2/3 cup milk
1/2 cup unprocessed natural bran
2 tbsp brown sugar, pkd
1 tbsp cooking oil
1/4 tsp baking soda
1/8 tsp salt
1 1/3 cups Ranch House Baking mix

Beat egg in medium bowl. Stir in milk, bran, brown sugar, oil, baking soda and salt. Let stand 30 minutes. Add baking mix. Stir quickly with a spoon until mixed, but still a little lumpy. Scrape bowl with a rubber spatula. Spoon batter into greased 2 3/4- inch muffin-pan cups, filling 2/3 full.

Bake at 400° 15 to 17 minutes or until center tests done. makes 6 muffins.

BUTTERMILK MUFFINS

2 1/4 cups Ranch House Baking Mix
2 1/2 tbsp sugar
2 1/2 tbsp butter or margarine, softened
1 egg
2/3 cups buttermilk
1 tbsp water

Place baking mix and sugar into medium bowl. Cut in butter with a pastry blender until mixture is consistency of cornmeal. Beat egg in small bowl. Blend in buttermilk and water, then add to baking mix. Stir quickly with a spoon until mixed, but still a little lumpy. Scrape bowl with a rubber spatula. Spoon batter into greased 2 3/4-inch muffin-pan cups, filling 2/3 full.

Bake at 400° 15 minutes or until center tests done. Makes 10 muffins.

CHEESE MUFFINS

1 egg
3/4 cup milk
1 tsp sugar
2 1/4 cups Ranch House Baking mix
1 cup (4-oz) grated Cheddar cheese

Beat egg in medium bowl. Blend in milk and sugar. Add baking mix. Stir quickly with a spoon until mixed but still a little lumpy. Scrape bowl with a rubber spatula. Fold in cheese. Spoon batter into greased 2 3/4-inch muffin-pan cups, filling 2/3 full.

Bake at 400° 15 minutes or until center tests done. Makes 11 to 12 muffins.

CORN MUFFINS

1 cup Ranch House Baking Mix
1/3 cup Yellow cornmeal
1 tsp sugar
1/8 tsp baking soda
1 egg
2/3 cup buttermilk
1 tbsp cooking oil

Place baking mix, cornmeal, sugar and baking soda into small bowl. Stir together with a pastry blender until well blended. Beat egg in another small bowl. Blend in buttermilk and oil, then add to baking mix. Beat at low speed just until smooth. Scrape bowl with a rubber spatula, stir 5 turns. Spoon batter into greased 2 3/4-inch muffin-pan cups, filling 2/3 to 3/4 full.

Bake at 425° 15 minutes or until center tests done. makes 6 muffins.

DATE MUFFINS

3/4 cup chopped dates, from an 8-oz pkg
1/8 tsp baking soda
3/4 cup boiling water
1/3 cup brown sugar, pkd
2 eggs, beaten
2 tbsp melted butter, cooled
1/2 tsp cinnamon
1/8 tsp nutmeg
2 1/4 cups Ranch House Baking Mix

Place dates into medium bowl. Add baking soda, boiling water and brown sugar. Stir until well mixed. Let stand 1 hour. Stir in eggs, butter and spices. Add baking mix. Stir quickly with a spoon until mixed, but still a little lumpy. Scrape bowl with a rubber spatula. Spoon batter into greased 2 3/4-inch muffin-pan cups, filling 2/3 full.

Bake at 400° 15 minutes or until center tests done. Makes 12 muffins.

GINGERBREAD MUFFINS

1/2 cup dark molasses
1/4 cup cooking oil
3 tbsp sugar
1 tsp ginger
1/2 tsp cinnamon
1/8 tsp each nutmeg and allspice
1/4 tsp baking soda
1/2 cup hot water
1 3/4 cups Ranch House Baking mix
1 egg, beaten

Place molasses, oil, sugar and spices into medium bowl. Stir baking soda into hot water. Add to molasses mixture. Beat at low speed until well mixed. Add baking mix. Beat at low speed 1 minute. Scrape bowl with a rubber spatula. Add egg. Beat at low speed 1 minute. Scrape bowl. Pour batter into greased 2 3/4-inch muffin-pan cups, filling 3/4 full.

Bake at 375° 15 to 17 minutes or until center tests done. Makes 8 muffins.

GOLDEN EGG MUFFINS

4 egg yolks
2 1/2 tbsp sugar
2 tsp water
2/3 cups milk
2 tbsp cooking oil
2 1/4 cups Ranch House Baking mix

Beat egg yolks, sugar and water in medium bowl at high speed 2 minutes. Blend in milk and oil at low speed. Add baking mix. Stir quickly with a spoon until mixed, but still a little lumpy. Scrape bowl with a rubber spatula. (Batter will be thinner than as for plain muffins.) Spoon into greased 2 3/4-inch muffin-pan cups, filling 3/4 full.

Bake at 400° 15 minutes or until center tests done. Makes 8 muffins.

HONEY BRAN MUFFINS

2 eggs
1 cup plus 2 tbsp milk
1 cup bran cereal
1/4 cup honey
3 tbsp wheat germ, plain or toasted
2 tbsp cooking oil
1/4 tsp baking soda
1/8 tsp salt
2 1/4 cups Ranch House baking mix

Beat eggs in medium bowl. Stir in milk, bran, honey, wheat germ, oil, baking soda and salt. Let stand 30 minutes. Add baking mix. Stir quickly with a spoon until mixed, but still a little lumpy. Scrape bowl with a rubber spatula. Spoon batter into greased 2 3/4-inch muffin-pan cups, filling 2/3 full.

Bake at 400° 15 to 17 minutes or until center tests done. Makes 12 muffins.

JAM MUFFINS

2 1/4 cups Ranch House Baking mix
1/4 cups brown sugar, pkd
1/8 tsp each cinnamon and ground coriander
2 tbsp butter or margarine, softened
1 egg
3/4 cups milk
10 tbsp boysenberry jam

Coat ten 2 3/4-inch muffin-pan cups with non-stick vegetable spray; set aside.

Place baking mix, brown sugar and spices into medium bowl. Cut in butter with a pastry blender until mixture is consistency of cornmeal. Beat egg in small bowl. Blend in milk, then add to baking mix. Stir quickly with a spoon until mixed, but still a little lumpy. Scrape bowl with a rubber spatula. Grease prepared pan with vegetable shortening. Spoon batter into cups, filling 1/4 full. Top with 1 tablespoon jam. Spoon remaining batter over jam, dividing evenly. Carefully spread batter with the back of a teaspoon to make an even layer.

Bake at 400° 15 minutes or until center tests done. Let stand 1 minute. Loosen edges with a small sharp knife, then invert muffins onto a foil covered baking sheet. Makes 10 muffins.

LEMON MUFFINS

BATTER
2 1/4 cups Ranch House Baking Mix
3/4 cup sugar
2 tbsp butter, softened
1 egg
1/2 cup water
1/4 cup lemon juice
1/2 tsp lemon extract

LEMON GLAZE
1/4 cup sugar
2 tbsp lemon juice
2 tbsp hot water

BATTER: Place baking mix and sugar into medium bowl. Stir with spoon to blend. Cut in butter with a pastry blender until mixture is consistency of cornmeal. Beat egg in small bowl. Blend in water, lemon juice and extract, then add to baking mix. Stir quickly with a spoon until mixed, but still a little lumpy. Scrape bowl with a rubber spatula. Spoon batter into greased and floured on bottom 2 3/4-inch muffin-pan cups, filling 2/3 full.

Bake at 400° 15 minutes or until center tests done. Spoon 1 1/2 teaspoons warm glaze over top of each muffin. Let stand 5 minutes before removing muffins from pan. Makes 10 muffins.

LEMON GLAZE: Place sugar, lemon juice and hot water into small saucepan. Stir over low heat until sugar dissolves and mixture is hot. Cool to lukewarm.

MAPLE BRAN MUFFINS

534

1 egg
2/3 cup milk
1/2 cup unprocessed natural bran
1/4 cup maple syrup
2 tbsp cooking oil
1/2 tsp maple extract
1/4 tsp baking soda
1/8 tsp salt
1 2/3 cups Ranch House Baking Mix

Beat egg in medium bowl. Stir in milk, bran, maple syrup, oil, extract, baking soda and salt. Let stand 30 minutes. Add baking mix. Stir quickly with a spoon until mixed, but still a little lumpy. Scrape bowl with a rubber spatula. Spoon batter into greased 2 3/4-inch muffin-pan cups, filling 2/3 full.

Bake at 400° 15 to 17 minutes or until center tests done. Makes 8 muffins.

MEXICAN CORN MUFFINS

1 cup Ranch House Baking Mix
1/3 cup stone ground yellow cornmeal
1/4 tsp chili powder
1/8 tsp cumin powder
1/8 tsp baking soda
1 egg, beaten
1/2 cup plus 2 tbsp buttermilk
1 tbsp cooking oil
1/4 cups deseeded minced green chilies

Place baking mix, cornmeal, chili powder, cumin powder and baking soda into small bowl. Stir together with a pastry blender until well blended. Add beaten egg, buttermilk and oil. Beat at low speed just until smooth. Add minced chilies. Scrape bowl with a rubber spatula, stir 10 turns to distribute chilies. Spoon batter into 6 greased 2 3/4-inch muffin-pan cups, dividing batter evenly.

Bake at 425° 15 to 18 minutes or until center tests done. Makes 6 muffins.

ORANGE MUFFINS

536

TOPPING

1/4 cup sugar

2 tsp Orange flavored instant breakfast drink powder

1/4 tsp cinnamon

1/8 tsp nutmeg

1/3 cup orange juice

BATTER

1 egg

3/4 cup orange juice

1/3 cup brown sugar, firmly pkd

2 tbsp melted butter, cooled

1/2 tsp cinnamon

1/8 tsp nutmeg

grated rind of 1 small orange

2 1/4 cups Ranch House Baking Mix

TOPPING: Combine sugar, orange powder,
cinnamon and nutmeg in small custard
cup; set aside. Set orange juice aside.

BATTER: Beat egg in medium bowl.
Blend in orange juice, brown sugar, butter,
spices and orange rind. Add baking mix.
Stir quickly with a spoon until mixed,
but still a little lumpy. Scrape bowl
with a rubber spatula. Spoon batter into
greased 2 3/4-inch muffin-pan cups,
filling 2/3 full. Sprinkle 1 teaspoon of the sugar mixture
over batter in each cup. (Reserve re-

maining topping :)

Bake at 400° 15 minutes or until center tests done. Drizzle 1 1/2 teaspoons of the reserved orange juice over tops of each muffin. Sprinkle with 1/4 teaspoon of the reserved topping. Let stand 5 minutes before removing muffins from pan. Makes 10 muffins.

ORANGE BRAN MUFFINS

2 eggs
1 cup orange juice
1 cup bran cereal
1/4 cups dark molasses
2 tbsp cooking oil
1/4 tsp baking soda
1/8 tsp salt
grated rind of 1 medium orange
2 1/4 cups Ranch House Baking Mix

Beat eggs in medium bowl. Stir in orange juice, bran, molasses, oil, soda, salt and grated rind. Let stand 30 minutes. Add baking mix. Stir quickly with a spoon until mixed, but still a little lumpy. Scrape bowl with a rubber spatula. Spoon batter into greased 2 3/4-inch muffin-pan cups, filling 2/3 full.

Bake at 400° 15 to 17 minutes or until center tests done. Makes 12 muffins.

TOPPING
1/2 cup sugar
1 1/2 tbsp Orange flavored instant breakfast drink powder
7 tbsp butter

BATTER
2 1/4 cups Ranch House Baking Mix
1/3 cup sugar
2 tbsp butter, softened
1 egg
3/4 cup orange juice
1/2 tsp orange extract

TOPPING: Combine sugar and orange powder in small shallow bowl; set aside. Melt butter in small saucepan; set aside.

BATTER: Place baking mix and sugar into medium bowl. Cut in butter with a pastry blender until mixture is consistency of cornmeal. Beat egg in small bowl. Blend in orange juice and extract, then add to baking mix. Stir quickly with a spoon until mixed, but still a little lumpy. Scrape bowl with a rubber spatula. Spoon batter into greased 2 3/4-inch muffin-pan cups, filling 2/3 to 3/4 full.

Bake at 400° 15 minutes or until center tests done. Cool 5 minutes. Loosen edges with a small sharp knife, then invert onto a foil covered baking sheet.

Dip each muffin into the melted butter in saucepan, coating all sides. Place muffin into topping mixture. With a teaspoon pour topping over muffin until coated on all sides. Place muffin back on baking sheet. Serve warm, or muffins may be served cold as a snack, with coffee or a glass of milk. Makes 9 muffins.

2 1/4 cups Ranch House Baking Mix
1/4 cup brown sugar, pkd
1/4 tsp nutmeg
2 tbsp butter, softened
1 egg
3/4 cup milk
1/2 cup chopped pecans

Place baking mix, brown sugar and nutmeg into medium bowl. Cut in butter with a pastry blender until mixture is consistency of cornmeal. Beat egg in small bowl. Blend in milk, then add to baking mix. Stir quickly with a spoon until mixed, but still a little lumpy. Add pecans. Scrape bowl with a rubber spatula, stir a few turns to distribute pecans. Spoon batter into greased 2 3/4-inch muffin-pan cups, filling 2/3 full.

Bake at 400° 15 minutes or until center tests done. makes 10 muffins.

PUMPKIN MUFFINS

2 eggs
1 cup canned pumpkin, from a 1-lb can
3/4 cup brown sugar, pkd
2 tbsp cooking oil
2 tsp pumpkin pie spice
1 tsp cinnamon
1/4 tsp baking soda
2 Tbsp hot water
2 1/2 cups Ranch House Baking Mix

Beat eggs in medium bowl. Add pumpkin, brown sugar, oil, pumpkin pie spice and cinnamon. Blend well at low speed. Combine baking soda and hot water. Blend into pumpkin mixture at low speed. Add baking mix. Beat at medium speed 1/2 minute. Scrape bowl with a rubber spatula, stir 10 turns. Spoon batter into greased 2 3/4-inch muffin-pan cups, filling 3/4 full.

Bake at 400° 15 to 17 minutes or until center tests done. Makes 12 muffins.

SPOONBREAD MUFFINS

1 cup hot water
1/4 tsp salt
1/3 cup quick grits
2 tbsp cooking oil
2/3 cup milk
2 eggs
2 cups Ranch House Baking Mix
1 tsp baking powder
1 tsp sugar
1/4 tsp baking soda

Bring hot water and salt to boiling in medium saucepan. Slowly stir in grits; cook and stir over medium heat until a thick mush forms. Remove saucepan from heat. Stir in oil. Gradually stir in milk; let stand 10 minutes. Add eggs, beat at medium speed 2 minutes. Combine baking mix, baking powder, sugar and baking soda in small bowl, then add to grits mixture. Stir with beaters to dampen, beat at low speed just until mixed. Scrape bowl with a rubber spatula. Spoon batter into greased 2 3/4-inch muffin-pan cups, filling 2/3 full.

Bake at 425° 20 to 22 minutes until golden brown. Muffins will still test a little moist at center. Makes 10.

STREUSEL MUFFINS

TOPPING
6 tbsp butter or margarine
3/4 cup graham cracker crumbs
6 tbsp finely chopped walnuts
1/3 cup plus 1 tbsp brown sugar, pkd
1 1/2 tsp cinnamon

BATTER
2 1/4 cups Ranch House Baking mix
2 1/2 tbsp sugar
2 tbsp butter or margarine, softened
1 egg
3/4 cup milk

TOPPING: melt butter in small saucepan over low heat. Remove from heat. Stir in graham cracker crumbs and chopped walnuts. Add brown sugar and cinnamon. Stir until well mixed; set aside.

Coat ten 2 3/4-inch muffin-pan cups with non-stick vegetable spray; set aside.

BATTER: Place baking mix and sugar into medium bowl. Cut in butter with a pastry blender until mixture is consistency of cornmeal. Beat egg in small bowl. Blend in milk, then add to baking mix. Stir quickly with a spoon until mixed, but still a little lumpy. Scrape bowl with a rubber spatula. Grease prepared pan with vegetable shortening. Spoon batter into cups, filling a scant 1/4 full.

Sprinkle with 2 tablespoons topping. Lightly press down with fingers to make an even layer. Spoon remaining batter over topping, dividing evenly. Sprinkle 2 tablespoons topping over batter. Lightly press down with fingers to make an even layer. Place pan on baking sheet to catch spills.

Bake at 400° 15 minutes or until center tests done. Let stand 2 minutes. Loosen edges of muffins with a small sharp knife. Invert onto a foil covered baking sheet. By hand turn muffins, placing top side up. Makes 10 muffins.

SUGAR 'N SPICE MUFFINS

TOPPING
1/2 cup sugar
1 1/2 tsp cinnamon
7 tbsp butter

BATTER
2 1/4 cups Ranch House Baking mix
1/4 cup sugar
1/2 tsp cinnamon
1/8 tsp each nutmeg and mace
2 tbsp butter, softened
1 egg
3/4 cup milk

TOPPING: Combine sugar and cinnamon in small shallow bowl; set aside. Melt butter in small saucepan; set aside.

BATTER: Place baking mix, sugar and spices into medium bowl. Cut in butter with pastry blender until mixture is consistency of cornmeal. Beat egg in small bowl. Blend in milk, then add to baking mix. Stir quickly with a spoon until mixed, but still a little lumpy. Scrape bowl with a rubber spatula. Spoon batter into greased 2 3/4-inch muffin-pan cups, filling 2/3 to 3/4 full.

Bake at 400° 15 minutes or until center tests done. Cool 5 minutes. Loosen edges with a small sharp knife, then invert onto a foil covered baking sheet. Dip each muffin into the melted butter in saucepan, coating all sides. Place muffin into topping mixture. With a teaspoon pour topping over muffin until coated on all sides. Place back on baking sheet. Serve warm, or muffins may be served cold as a snack, with coffee or a glass of milk. Makes 9 muffins.

WALNUT MUFFINS

1 egg
3/4 cup milk
1/4 cup brown sugar, firmly pkd
1 tbsp granulated sugar
2 tbsp melted butter, cooled
1/8 tsp each cinnamon and nutmeg
2 1/4 cups Ranch House Baking mix
1/2 cup chopped walnuts

Beat egg in medium bowl. Blend in milk, brown and granulated sugar, butter and spices. Add baking mix. Stir quickly with a spoon until mixed, but still a little lumpy. Add walnuts. Scrape bowl with a rubber spatula, stir a few turns to distribute walnuts. Spoon batter into greased 2 3/4-inch muffin-pan cups, filling 2/3 full.

Bake at 400° 15 minutes or until center tests done. Makes 10 muffins.

The aroma of bacon or sausage frying, and pancakes cooking to golden perfection is bliss for the pancake lovers. A perfect breakfast to them is a stack of golden wheels on a plate, ready to be bathed in maple syrup, honey or a special sauce.

If a "stack of wheats" is the usual breakfast fare in your household, break away from the mundane and serve up a surprise. Try spicy Gingerbread Pancakes, Walnut Pancakes, Apple or Sausage Pancakes. For a special treat serve Yorkshire Pancake with one of the delicious sauces or toppings. This unusual pancake is baked in a skillet and rises high above the rim of the pan.

Heating the griddle to the right temperature is of utmost importance when cooking pancakes. It is advisable to cook one or two small test pancakes to determine if the griddle is heated to correct temperature. An electric griddle simplifies the task of maintaining the correct temperature. Lacking one, experiment with a regular griddle or large skillet until you can correctly regulate the amount of heat needed to cook the pancakes. Pour batter onto hot greased griddle, spreading a little with the back of a tablespoon if a thinner pancake is desired. Don't crowd the pancakes on the griddle for they will be difficult to turn. When the top is full of bubbles, about 2 1/2 to 3 minutes, the underside should be golden brown. Loosen the edges of each pancake with a pancake turner before turning to brown underside. Turn only once. When done remove to a heated platter or serving plates, stacking about 4 in each pile.

Store leftover pancakes in refrigerator 3 or 4 days, or wrap well in plastic wrap and freeze 3 months. To reheat pancakes, thaw first if frozen. Wrap stacked pancakes in double thickness of waxed paper. Dampen a double thickness of paper towels, then place in center of a length of foil about 24 inches long. Place the package of pancakes on damp towels, then wrap in foil. Heat in oven 325° 18 to 25 minutes, depending upon the number of pancakes being heated.

APPLE PANCAKES

1 1/2 cups Ranch House Baking mix
3 tbsp sugar
1/2 tsp cinnamon
1/4 tsp each baking soda and nutmeg
2/3 cup milk
2 eggs, beaten
2 tbsp cooking oil
1 1/2 cups (2 medium Golden Delicious) medium
  to finely chopped apples, undrained

APPLE SYRUP
3 tbsp butter or margarine
1/2 cup syrup
1/2 cup apple juice or cider
1/4 cup brown sugar, pkd
1/4 tsp cinnamon extract

Place baking mix, sugar, cinnamon,
baking soda and nutmeg into a 4-cup measure
with a pouring spout. Stir with a fork to
blend. Add milk, eggs and oil. Stir with
beaters to dampen, beat at medium speed
15 seconds. Scrape container with a rubber
spatula. Fold in apples until well blended.
Let stand 15 minutes. Pour 1/4 cup batter for
each pancake onto greased griddle heated
to 360°. Cook pancakes 5 minutes on
each side until golden brown, and apples
are tender. Serve with warm Apple Syrup.
makes one dozen 4-inch pancakes.

APPLE SYRUP: Melt butter in small
saucepan over low heat. Add syrup,

apple juice, brown sugar and extract.
Bring to boiling over medium heat, then
lower heat until mixture is simmering.
Cook, uncovered, 5 minutes. Cover. Let
stand until lukewarm. Makes about 1 1/4
cups.

BLUEBERRY PANCAKES

1 1/2 cups Ranch House Baking mix
3 tbsp sugar
1/8 tsp each cinnamon and nutmeg
1 cup milk
2 egg yolks
3 tbsp melted butter or margarine, cooled
3/4 cups washed, well drained fresh blueberries or
    3/4 cups unsweetened frozen blueberries, unthawed
2 egg whites

Place baking mix, sugar and spices
into a 4-cup measure with a pouring spout.
Stir with a fork to blend. Add milk and egg
yolks. Stir with beaters to dampen, beat at
medium speed 15 seconds. Scrape container
with a rubber spatula. Stir in melted butter.
Fold in blueberries; set aside. Beat egg whites
in medium bowl until soft peaks form. Fold in
1/4 of the batter, then gradually fold egg white
mixture into remaining batter. Pour 1/4 cup
batter for each pancake onto hot greased
griddle. Cook until lightly browned on
both sides. Gently stir batter before pouring
each batch of pancakes. Spread batter if
thinner pancakes are desired. Makes ten
to twelve 4-inch pancakes.

1 1/2 cups Ranch House Baking mix
1/4 cup sweetened chocolate beverage powder (see note)
1/8 tsp baking soda
2/3 cups buttermilk
1/4 cup evaporated milk
2 eggs, beaten
3 tbsp melted butter or margarine, cooled

Place baking mix, chocolate powder
and baking soda into a 4-cup measure
with a pouring spout. Stir with a
pastry blender until well mixed. Add
buttermilk, evaporated milk and eggs.
Stir with beaters to dampen, beat at
medium speed 15 seconds. Scrape container
with a rubber spatula. Stir in melted
butter. Pour 3 tablespoons batter for
each pancake onto hot greased
griddle. Cook until lightly browned
on both sides. Makes one dozen 3 1/2-
inch pancakes.

NOTE: 2 tablespoons cocoa powder and 3 tablespoons sugar may be used instead of the
chocolate beverage powder.

2 1/2 cups Ranch House Baking mix
1 1/4 cups buttermilk
1 tbsp sugar
2 eggs, beaten
1/4 tsp baking soda
1 tbsp warm water
3 tbsp melted butter or margarine, cooled

Place baking mix, buttermilk and sugar into a 4-cup measure with a pouring spout. Stir with beaters to dampen, beat at medium speed 15 seconds. Scrape container with a rubber spatula. Loosely cover with foil. Let stand at room temperature overnight. (Batter may stand up to 12 hours.) The next morning: Stir in beaten eggs. Combine baking soda and warm water in a small custard cup. Stir into batter. Blend in melted butter. If batter needs thinning, add more buttermilk. Pour 1/4 cup batter for each pancake onto hot greased griddle. Cook until golden brown on both sides. Makes one dozen 5-inch pancakes.

DELUXE BUTTERMILK PANCAKES

1 1/2 cups Ranch House Baking mix
2 tsp sugar
1/8 tsp baking soda
1 cup buttermilk
2 eggs, beaten
3 tbsp melted butter or margarine, cooled

Place baking mix, sugar and baking soda into a 4-cup measure with a pouring spout. Stir with a fork until blended. Add buttermilk and eggs. Stir with beaters to dampen, beat at medium speed 15 seconds. Scrape container with a rubber spatula. Stir in melted butter. Pour 1/4 cup batter for each pancake onto hot greased griddle. Cook until golden brown on both sides. Makes eight 5-inch pancakes.

GINGERBREAD PANCAKES

1 1/2 cups Ranch House Baking Mix
1 tsp pumpkin pie spice
3/4 tsp cinnamon
1/2 tsp ginger
1/8 tsp baking soda
1 cup buttermilk
1/4 cup dark molasses
2 egg yolks
3 tbsp melted butter or margarine, cooled
2 egg whites
1/4 tsp cream of tartar

Place baking mix, spices and baking soda into a 4-cup measure with a pouring spout. Stir with a fork until blended. Add buttermilk, molasses and egg yolks. Stir with beaters to dampen, beat at medium speed 15 seconds. Scrape container with a rubber spatula. Stir in melted butter; set aside. Beat egg whites and cream of tartar in medium bowl until soft peaks form. Fold in 1/4 of the batter, then gradually fold egg white mixture into remaining batter. Pour 1/4 cup batter for each pancake onto hot greased griddle. Cook until golden brown on both sides. Gently stir batter before pouring each batch of pancakes. Serve with warm Rum Molasses Syrup. (P-558) makes ten 4 1/2-inch pancakes.

1 cup Pumpkin Pie mix, from a 21-oz can
1/4 cup dark molasses
2 egg yolks
2 tbsp cooking oil
2 cups Ranch House Baking mix
1 cup milk
2 egg whites
1/4 tsp cream of tartar

RUM MOLASSES SYRUP
1/4 cup butter or margarine
1 cup syrup
3 tbsp dark molasses
2 tbsp light or dark rum
1/2 tsp each rum and brandy extract

Beat pie mix, molasses, egg yolks and oil in a 4-cup measure with a pouring spout at low speed until well blended. Add baking mix and milk. Stir with beaters to dampen, beat at medium speed 15 seconds. Scrape container with a rubber spatula; set aside. Beat egg whites and cream of tartar in medium bowl until soft peaks form. Fold in 1/4 of the batter, then gradually fold egg white mixture into remaining batter. Pour 1/4 cup batter for each pancake onto hot greased griddle. Cook until golden brown on both sides. Serve with warm Rum molasses Syrup. makes one dozen 4 1/2-inch pancakes.

RUM MOLASSES SYRUP: melt butter in small saucepan over low heat. Stir in remaining ingredients. Heat, uncovered, over medium heat until small bubbles appear around edges of pan; do not boil. Cover. Let stand until lukewarm. makes 1 1/2 cups.

QUICK PANCAKES

2 eggs
3 tbsp cooking oil
1 tbsp sugar
1 1/2 cups milk
2 cups Ranch House Baking mix

Beat eggs, oil and sugar in a 4-cup measure with a pouring spout at high speed 2 minutes. Blend in milk at low speed. Add baking mix. Stir with beaters to dampen, beat at medium speed 20 seconds. Scrape container with a rubber spatula. Pour 1/4 cup batter for each pancake onto hot greased griddle. Cook until golden brown on both sides. Makes ten 5-inch pancakes.

QUICK BUTTERMILK PANCAKES

2 eggs
1/4 cup cooking oil
1 tbsp sugar
1 1/3 cups buttermilk
1/4 cup evaporated milk
1/4 tsp baking soda
1 tsp warm water
2 cups Ranch House Baking mix

Beat eggs, oil and sugar in a 4-cup measure with a pouring spout. Blend in buttermilk and evaporated milk. Dissolve soda in the warm water. Blend into the buttermilk mixture. Add baking mix. Stir with beaters to dampen, beat at medium speed 20 seconds. Scrape container with a rubber spatula. Pour 1/4 cup batter for each pancake onto hot greased griddle. Cook until golden brown on both sides. Makes ten 5-inch pancakes.

SAUSAGE PANCAKES

1 1/2 cups Ranch House Baking Mix
1 tsp sugar
1/8 tsp baking soda
1 1/4 cups buttermilk
1 egg, beaten
1 tbsp cooking oil
2/3 cups cooked bulk pork sausage, finely
   crumbled, cooled

Place baking mix, sugar, baking soda, buttermilk, egg and oil into a 4-cup measure with a pouring spout. Stir with beaters to dampen, beat at medium speed 20 seconds. Scrape container with a rubber spatula. Stir in sausage until well blended. Pour 3 tablespoons batter for each pancake onto hot greased griddle. Cook until golden brown on both sides. Gently stir batter before pouring each batch of pancakes. Makes one dozen 3 1/2-inch pancakes.

SOUTHERN PANCAKES

1 2/3 cups Ranch House Baking mix
1 1/4 tsp baking soda
1 cup buttermilk
1/4 cup light cream
2 egg yolks
1/4 cup melted butter, cooled
2 egg whites
4 tsp sugar

Place baking mix and baking soda into a 4-cup measure with a pouring spout. Add buttermilk, cream and egg yolks. Stir with beaters to dampen, beat at medium speed 15 seconds. Scrape container with a rubber spatula. Stir in melted butter; set aside. Beat egg whites in medium bowl until foamy. Add sugar. Beat until soft peaks form. Fold in 1/4 of the batter, then gradually fold egg white mixture into remaining batter. Pour 1/3 cup batter for each pancake onto hot greased griddle. Cook until golden brown on both sides. Gently stir batter before pouring each batch of pancakes. Makes light 5-inch pancakes.

1 3/4 cups Ranch House Baking Mix
3/4 cup white or yellow stone ground cornmeal
1 tbsp sugar
1/4 tsp each baking soda, baking powder and salt
2 cups buttermilk
2 eggs, beaten
1/4 cup melted butter or margarine, cooled

Place baking mix, cornmeal, sugar, baking soda, baking powder and salt into a 4-cup measure with a pouring spout. Stir with a pastry blender until well mixed. Add buttermilk and eggs. Stir with beaters to dampen, beat at medium speed 20 seconds. Scrape container with a rubber spatula. Stir in melted butter. Pour 1/4 cup batter for each pancake onto hot greased griddle. Cook until golden brown on both sides. Makes 1 1/2 dozen 4-inch pancakes.

SWEDISH PANCAKES

1 1/2 cups Ranch House Baking mix
1 cup milk
2 large or 3 small eggs
1 tsp sugar
1/4 cups melted butter, cooled

Place baking mix, milk, eggs and sugar into electric blender container. Blend at low speed 20 seconds. Scrape sides of container with a rubber spatula. Add melted butter, blend at low speed 20 seconds. Pour batter into a 4-cup measure with a pouring spout. (Batter will be thin.) Let stand 30 minutes. Gently stir batter, then pour 2 tablespoons for each pancake onto hot greased griddle. Cook until pale golden on both sides. Gently stir batter before pouring each batch of pancakes. Serve with Boysenberry or Lingonberry syrup. Makes 1 1/2 dozen 3 1/2-inch pancakes.

1 1/2 cups Ranch House Baking Mix
1/2 cup ground walnuts
1 tbsp. sugar
1/4 tsp. cinnamon
1 cups milk
2 egg yolks
3 tbsp. melted butter or margarine, cooled
2 egg whites

Place baking mix, ground walnuts, sugar and cinnamon into a 4-cup measure with a pouring spout. Stir with a pastry blender until well mixed. Add milk and egg yolks. Stir with beaters to dampen, beat at medium speed 15 seconds. Scrape container with a rubber spatula. Stir in melted butter; set aside. Beat egg whites in medium bowl until soft peaks form. Fold in 1/4 of the batter, then gradually fold egg white mixture into remaining batter. Pour 3 1/2 tablespoons batter for each pancake onto hot greased griddle. Cook until golden brown on both sides. Gently stir batter before pouring each batch of pancakes. Spread batter if thinner pancakes are desired. Makes 1 dozen 4-inch pancakes.

<u>2 SERVINGS</u>

2 eggs
1/2 cup plus 2 tbsp Ranch House Baking Mix
1/2 cup milk
2 teaspoons butter for pan

<u>3 SERVINGS</u>

3 eggs
3/4 cup plus 2 tbsp Ranch House Baking Mix
3/4 cup milk
1 tablespoon butter for pan

PANCAKE TOPPINGS; recipes follow

BATTER: Place eggs, baking mix and milk into electric blender container. Beat at medium speed 1 minute. Scrape sides of container with a rubber spatula. Beat at medium speed 2 minutes.

2 SERVINGS: Heat an 8 1/2-inch (across top) heavy iron skillet over medium heat 7 minutes. Melt butter, tilting pan to coat sides and bottom. Turn heat off. Pour in batter. Bake at 450° 8 minutes. Lower heat to 350°. Bake 12 minutes longer until pancake rises high above rim of pan and turns golden brown. Slip pancake out of pan onto serving platter. (Center will sink.) Cut in half. Transfer to serving plates. Serve with desired topping. Recipe can be doubled to make 4 servings, baked in 2 skillets.

3 SERVINGS: Heat a 9 1/2-inch (across top) heavy iron skillet over medium heat 7 minutes. Melt butter, tilting pan to coat sides and bottom. Turn heat off. Pour in batter. Bake at 450° 8 minutes. Lower heat to 350°. Bake 17 to 20 minutes longer until pancake rises high above rim of pan and turns golden brown. Slip pancake out of pan onto serving platter. (Center will sink.) Cut into serving

portions. Transfer to serving plates. Serve with desired topping.

SAUSAGE TOPPING for 2 servings. Make 1 1/2 measures for 3 servings, and double the recipe for 4 servings.

2 tsp butter
4 brown and serve sausage links, cut into 1/4-inch rings
3/4 cup hot water
1 tsp instant chicken bouillon granules
2 tbsp instant flour
1/4 cup milk
pepper to taste

Fry sausage rings in butter in small saucepan over medium heat until lightly browned. Add hot water and bouillon. Bring to boiling. Combine flour and milk in a 1-cup measure. Gradually stir into boiling liquid. Lower heat until mixture is simmering. Cook and stir until gravy thickens. Add pepper to taste. Serve hot.

STROGANOFF TOPPING for 2 servings. Make 1 1/2 measures for 3 servings, and double the recipe for 4 servings.

1/2 pound lean ground beef
1/2 cup cream of mushroom soup, from 10 3/4-oz can
1/2 tbsp catsup
1/4 tsp each Worcestershire sauce and onion powder
1/8 tsp each garlic salt and pepper
1/3 cup sour cream

Fry ground beef in small skillet over medium-to-high heat until red color leaves meat, breaking up chunks as it cooks. Spoon off fat. Continue cooking until meat is lightly browned. Add mushroom soup, catsup, Worcestershire and seasonings. Cook and stir over low heat 5 minutes. Add sour cream.

Cook and stir 2 minutes; do not boil.

Serve hot.

ORANGE SYRUP for 2 servings. Make 1 1/2 measures for 3 servings, and double the recipe for 4 servings.

1 tbsp butter
1/3 cup light corn syrup
1/4 cup orange juice
1 tbsp sugar
1 1/2 tsp orange flavored instant breakfast drink powder

Melt butter in small saucepan over low heat. Stir in syrup, orange juice, sugar and orange powder. Bring to boiling over medium heat, stirring occasionally. Lower heat until mixture is simmering. Cook, uncovered and without stirring 1 minute. Serve warm.

HONEY SYRUP for 2 servings. Make 1 1/2 measures for 3 servings, and double the recipe for 4 servings.

1 tbsp butter
3 tbsp hot water
6 tbsp honey

Place butter and hot water into small saucepan. Heat over medium heat until butter melts. Add honey. Cook and stir until mixture comes to boiling. Lower heat until mixture is simmering. Cook, uncovered and without stirring, 1 minute. Serve warm.

FRUIT TOPPING WITH MARNY SAUCE for 2 servings. Make 1 1/2 measures for 3 servings, and double the recipe for 4 servings.

1 1/4 cups fresh sliced strawberries or thinly sliced peaches
1/4 cup sour cream

2 tbsp honey
2 tbsp confectioners' sugar
1/2 tsp brandy extract
1/4 tsp each rum, orange and vanilla extract
6 tbsp heavy whipping cream

Chill fruit while preparing sauce. Place sour cream, honey, confectioners' sugar and extracts into small bowl. Beat at low speed until well blended; set aside. Beat cream at high speed in another small bowl until stiff. Gradually fold in sour cream mixture. Spoon 1/2 of the fruit over each serving of hot Yorkshire Pancake. Top with Mammy Sauce.

Yorkshire Pancake can be served as an entree for breakfast, lunch or supper. Or serve for dessert with fruit and Mammy Sauce.

Give careful attention to measuring and mixing the ingredients, as in making popovers. If the pancake should fail to rise to its fullest height, it still will be good enough to serve.

4 slices COTTAGE CHEESE OR POTATO BREAD
cut 1/2-inch thick (p- 114 p- 121)

2 eggs
1/3 cups milk
2 tbsp butter for frying

ORANGE HONEY SYRUP
1 tbsp butter
1/3 cups orange juice
1/3 cups honey

Slightly beat eggs in small bowl. Blend
in milk at low speed. Lay bread slices on
a small rimmed baking sheet. Spoon with
1/2 of the egg mixture. Turn with pancake
turner. Spoon with remaining egg mixture,
dividing evenly. Let stand 1/2 minute. Melt
butter in large skillet over medium heat.
Transfer bread slices to skillet with a
pancake turner. Cook until golden brown
on both sides. Serve with warm Orange Honey
Syrup. makes 4 servings.

ORANGE HONEY SYRUP: Melt butter in small
saucepan. Stir in orange juice and honey.
Bring to boiling over medium heat, then
lower heat until mixture is simmering.
Cook, uncovered, 5 minutes. Cover. Let
stand until lukewarm.

4 slices COTTAGE CHEESE OR POTATO BREAD
   cut 1/2-inch thick. (P- 114   P- 121)
2 tbsp butter
1/4 cups orange juice
1 tbsp sugar
2 eggs
1/3 cups milk

ORANGE TOPPING
2 tbsp sugar
1 1/2 tsp Orange flavored instant breakfast drink powder
1/4 tsp cinnamon
1/8 tsp nutmeg

Melt butter in a baking pan just large
enough to hold bread slices; set aside. Combine
orange juice and 1 tablespoon sugar in a 1-cup
measure; set aside. Slightly beat eggs in small
bowl. Blend in milk. Lay bread slices on a
small rimmed baking sheet. Spoon with 1/2 of
the egg mixture. Turn with pancake turner.
Spoon with remaining egg mixture. Let stand 1/2
minute. Transfer bread to buttered baking pan
with pancake turner. Pour 1/2 of the orange
juice mixture around the edges of pan. Sprinkle
topping over bread, dividing evenly.

Bake at 350° 15 minutes. Pour remaining
orange juice around the edges of pan. Continue
baking until bread absorbs the orange juice,
around 10 to 12 minutes. Serve with orange
marmalade. Makes 4 servings.

ORANGE TOPPING: Combine ingredients in
small custard cups, stirring until well blended.

1 egg
3/4 cups plus 2 tbsp buttermilk
1/4 cups sugar
2 tbsp cooking oil
1/2 tsp cinnamon
1/8 tsp each baking soda, nutmeg and allspice
1 2/3 cups Ranch House Baking mix
2 medium to large Golden Delicious apples
3 tbsp vegetable shortening for frying

TOPPING
1/4 cup sugar
1 tsp cinnamon

Beat egg in medium bowl. Blend in buttermilk, sugar, oil, cinnamon, baking soda, nutmeg and allspice. Add baking mix. Stir with beaters to dampen, beat at medium speed 20 seconds. Scrape bowl with a rubber spatula, stir 10 turns; set aside. Peel, core then cut each apple into six 1/4-inch slices. Heat griddle to 320°. Add 2 tablespoons of the shortening. Dip apple slices into batter. Place on greased griddle, spacing about 2 inches apart. Cook 15 minutes. Sprinkle a rounded 1/4 teaspoon topping over each fritter. Lower griddle temperature to 300°. Turn fritters. Add remaining shortening to griddle. Sprinkle each fritter with a rounded 1/4 teaspoon topping. Cook 10 minutes, then loosely cover griddle with foil. Continue cooking fritters until tender, about 8 minutes longer. Serve with maple syrup. Makes 1 dozen fritters.

TOPPING: Combine sugar and cinnamon in a small custard cup.

NOTE: If griddle is not large enough to cook fritters all at once, after cooking first batch transfer to a foil lined baking pan. Loosely cover pan with foil. Keep fritters warm in 200° oven. or 1 griddle and 1 electric skillet may be used to cook fritters all at once.

PRESS-IN PASTRY

Pastry shells are easy to make, using the press-in method. If you enjoy eating home-baked pies, but avoid making them because you dislike tussling with pastry that sticks, breaks or crumbles, switch to the press-in method. No rolling of the dough is required, a task even some experienced cooks find exasperating at times. There is a variety of press-in pastry to choose from, for desserts and entrees. The Rich Chocolate Press-In Pastry makes a delicious crisp cookie-like shell, perfect for ice cream pie, cream pies and other desserts. Sour Cream Press-In Pastry is great for entrees. The Yeast Press-In Pastry is versatile. You can press the dough into the pan to form a shell, or roll out for turnovers, appetizers and casserole toppings. Follow the recipe directions carefully to ensure success with making the press-in pastry shells.

NOTE: PRESS-IN PASTRY is not suitable for making two-crust pies such as apple, berry or cherry. If making a one-crust fruit pie, the shell should be pre-baked and cooled before spooning in the cooled cooked filling.

9-inch SHELL
1 1/2 cups Ranch House Baking mix
2 tbsp sugar
3 tbsp butter, softened
2 tbsp cold water

Place baking mix and sugar into medium bowl. Cut in butter with a pastry blender until coarse particles form. Gradually sprinkle cold water over mixture, blending together with a fork; add just enough water to form a pliable dough. Round up into a smooth ball. Place tablespoons of dough at close intervals on bottom and around sides of a 9-inch glass pie pan. Press with fingers to form a shell, then mold pastry upwards around the rim to form a standing collar 1/2-inch high; flute.

If recipe specifies a baked shell, don't prick pastry. Bake at 400° 7 minutes. Examine shell for any puffed up areas. With the back of a tablespoon gently press flat. Continue baking 5 to 6 minutes longer or until a light golden color. Do not overbake. Cool shell in pan on rack before filling.

If recipe specifies unbaked shell, don't prick pastry. Spoon in filling. Bake as directed in recipe. Makes one 9-inch shell.

BUTTERMILK PRESS-IN PASTRY

9-inch SHELL

1 1/2 cups Ranch House Baking Mix
3 tbsp plus 1 tsp Vegetable shortening
3 1/2 tbsp buttermilk

Place baking mix into medium bowl. Cut in shortening with a pastry blender until coarse particles form. Add buttermilk all at once. Stir with a fork until a pliable dough forms. If dough feels a little stiff, work in a small amount of buttermilk. Round up into a smooth ball. Place tablespoons of dough at close intervals on bottom and around sides of a 9-inch glass pie pan. Press with fingers to form a shell, then mold pastry upwards around the rim to form a standing collar 1/2-inch high; flute.

If recipe specifies a baked shell, don't prick pastry. Bake at 400° 7 minutes. Examine shell for any puffed up areas. With the back of a tablespoon gently press flat. Continue baking 5 to 7 minutes longer or until a light golden color. Do not overbake. Cool shell on rack before filling.

If recipe specifies an unbaked shell, don't prick pastry. Spoon in filling. Bake as directed in recipe. Makes one 9-inch shell.

CHOCOLATE PRESS-IN PASTRY

<u>8 - inch shell</u>
1 cup Ranch House Baking mix
2 1/2 tbsp sugar
2 tbsp cocoa
2 1/2 tbsp Vegetable shortening
1 1/2 tbsp cold water

<u>9-inch shell</u>
1 1/3 cups Ranch House Baking mix
2 1/2 tbsp sugar
2 tbsp cocoa
2 tbsp plus 2 tsp Vegetable shortening
2 tbsp cold water

<u>10-inch shell</u>
1 2/3 cups Ranch House Baking mix
3 tbsp sugar
2 1/2 tbsp cocoa
3 tbsp Vegetable shortening
2 tbsp plus 1 to 2 tsp cold water

Generously coat a glass pie pan in selected size with non-stick Vegetable spray; set aside.

PASTRY: Combine baking mix, sugar and cocoa in medium bowl. Cut in shortening with a pastry blender until coarse particles form. Gradually sprinkle cold water over mixture, blending together with a fork; add just enough water to form a pliable dough. Round up into a smooth ball. Place tablespoons of dough at close intervals on bottom and around sides of prepared pan. Press with fingers to form a shell, then mold pastry upwards around the rim to form a standing collar 1/2-inch high; flute.

If recipe specifies a baked shell, don't prick pastry. Bake at 375° 7 minutes. Examine shell for any puffed up areas. With the back of a tablespoon gently press flat. Continue baking 5 minutes longer or until lightly browned around the edges. Do not overbake. Cool shell on rack before filling.

If recipe specifies an unbaked shell, don't prick pastry. Spoon in filling. Bake as directed in recipe.

PRESS-IN PASTRY (BASIC)

<u>8-inch shell</u>
1 1/4 cups Ranch House Baking mix
3 tbsp Vegetable shortening
2 to 2 1/2 tbsp cold water

<u>9-inch shell</u>
1 1/2 cups Ranch House Baking mix
3 tbsp plus 1 tsp Vegetable shortening
2 1/2 to 3 tbsp cold water

<u>10-inch shell</u>
2 cups Ranch House Baking mix
1/4 cup plus 1/2 tbsp Vegetable shortening
3 to 3 1/2 tbsp cold water

Place baking mix into medium bowl. Cut in shortening with a pastry blender until coarse particles form. Gradually sprinkle cold water over mixture, blending together with a fork; add just enough water to form a pliable dough. Round up into a smooth ball. Place tablespoons of dough at close intervals on bottom and around sides of glass pie pan. Press with fingers to form a shell, then mold pastry upwards around the rim to form a standing collar 1/2-inch high;

flute.

If recipe specifies a baked shell, don't prick pastry. Bake at 450° 7 minutes. Examine shell for any puffed up areas. With the back of a tablespoon gently press flat. Continue baking 5 to 7 minutes longer or until a light golden color. Do not overbake. Cool shell on rack before filling.

If recipe specifies an unbaked shell, don't prick pastry. Spoon in filling. Bake as directed in recipe.

1 recipe PRESS-IN PASTRY for 10-inch shell (P-579)

TART SHELLS: Divide pastry into 4 equal pieces. Working with one portion at a time, place rounded teaspoonfuls of dough on bottom and around sides of 6-oz glass baking cups. Press with fingers to form a shell, then mold pastry upwards around the rim to form a standing collar ½-inch high; flute. Repeat with remaining pastry.

If recipe specifies baked shells, don't prick pastry. Bake at 500° 6 minutes. Examine shells for any puffed up areas. With the back of a teaspoon gently press flat. Continue baking 5 to 7 minutes longer or until a light golden color. Do not over-bake. Cool shells in cups on rock before filling.

If recipe specifies unbaked shells, don't prick pastry. Spoon in filling. Bake as directed in recipe. Makes 4 tart shells.

PRESS-IN PASTRY TOPPING

1 cup Ranch Baking mix
2 1/2 tbsp Vegetable shortening
1 1/2 tbsp cold water

Place baking mix into small bowl. Cut in shortening with a pastry blender until coarse particles form. Gradually sprinkle cold water over mixture, blending together with a fork. Add just enough water to form a pliable dough. Round up into a smooth ball. For un-baked pastry topping follow directions in recipe.

To prebake pastry, to top 1 hot casserole or dessert prepared in 8 or 9-inch square or round baking dish or pan, place pastry on a baking sheet. Press into desired shape. Don't prick pastry. Bake at 400° 7 to 8 minutes or until a light golden color. Do not over-bake. Cool 5 minutes. Lift pastry onto top of casserole or dessert just before serving.

To prebake pastry, to top 4 individual casseroles or desserts prepared in 10- oz glass baking dishes or 12-oz pottery baking dishes, divide pastry into 4 equal pieces. Roll into smooth balls between palms of hands. Place balls on a baking sheet about 4 1/2-inches apart. Press into 4 inch rounds. Bake at 400° 6 to 8 minutes or until a light golden color. Do not overbake. Cool 5 minutes. Lift pastry onto top of casserole or dessert just before serving.

NOTE: The pastry may be baked ahead, then

reheated on a baking sheet in 325°
oven 5 to 7 minutes, just before serving.

8-inch SHELL
1 cup plus 2 tbsp Ranch House Baking mix
1/4 cup sugar
2 tbsp cocoa
2 1/2 tbsp butter, softened
1 1/2 tbsp cold water

9-inch SHELL
1 1/3 cups Ranch House Baking mix
1/3 cup sugar
2 1/2 tbsp cocoa
3 tbsp butter, softened
1 3/4 tbsp cold water

10-inch SHELL
1 1/2 cups Ranch House Baking mix
1/3 cup plus 1 tbsp sugar
3 tbsp cocoa
3 tbsp butter, softened
2 tbsp cold water

PREPARE PAN: Foil-line a glass pie pan in selected size, extending foil 1 1/2-inches beyond rim. Trim uneven edges. Press foil against sides of pan. Heavily coat liner with non-stick vegetable spray; set aside.

PASTRY: Place baking mix, sugar and cocoa into medium bowl. Stir with a fork to blend. Cut in butter with a pastry blender until coarse particles form. Gradually sprinkle cold water over mixture, blending together with a fork; add just enough water to form a pliable dough. Round

585

up into a smooth ball. Place tablespoons of dough at close intervals on bottom and around sides of prepared pan. Press with fingers to form a shell, then mold pastry upwards around the rim to form a standing collar 1/2-inch high; flute. Release foil from sides of pan, bring it up beyond the pastry collar. Press the foil collar slightly inward around the pastry collar to hold it in place as it bakes. Don't prick pastry.

Bake at 375° 7 minutes. Examine shell for any puffed up areas. With the back of a tablespoon gently press flat. Continue baking 5 to 8 minutes longer until shell is lightly browned around the edges. Do not overbake. Cool shell in pan on rack until cold. Remove foil liner with shell from pan. Turn down edges of foil; carefully remove shell from foil, then slip back into pan. Spoon in filling as desired.

NOTE: This rich chocolate pastry is suitable for baked shells only. Use for cream pies, frozen desserts and other desserts. A little extra care in cutting is required to prevent pastry from breaking. To neatly cut into servings, use a sharp knife. Make short downward thrusts, then continue cutting in a gentle sawing motion through filling and crust.

2 cups Ranch House Baking mix
2 tbsp butter, softened
1 tbsp Vegetable shortening
1 1/2 tsp active dry yeast
1 tsp sugar
3 tbsp warm water
2 tbsp beaten egg
1 tbsp evaporated milk

Place baking mix into medium bowl. Cut in butter and shortening with a pastry blender until coarse particles form; set aside.

Stir together yeast, sugar and warm water in a 1-cup measure; let stand until bubbly, 5 to 10 minutes. Add to baking mix. Add beaten egg and evaporated milk. Stir with a spoon until dough leaves the sides of bowl. Continue stirring 2 minutes until smooth and pliable. Dough should be just soft enough to shape without crumbling if pressing into place, or crumbling or sticking if rolling out on a floured surface. If too dry, add a small amount of cold water. If too soft add a small amount of baking mix.

Shape, fill and bake as directed in individual recipes. The pastry may be used for desserts, sweet crescent rolls, appetizers and turnovers.

9-inch SHELL

1 1/2 cups Rand House Baking mix
3 tbsp Vegetable shortening
1/4 cup sour cream

Place baking mix into medium bowl. Cut in shortening with a pastry blender until coarse particles form. Add sour cream all at once. Stir with a fork until a pliable dough forms. If dough feels a little stiff, work in a small amount of sour cream. Round up into a smooth ball. Place tablespoons of dough at close intervals on bottom and around sides of a 9-inch glass pie pan. Press with fingers to form a shell, then mold pastry upwards around the rim to form a standing collar 1/2-inch high; flute.

If recipe specifies a baked shell, don't prick pastry. Bake at 400° 7 minutes. Examine shell for any puffed up areas. With the back of a tablespoon gently press flat. Continue baking 5 to 7 minutes longer or until a light golden color. Do not overbake. Cool shell on rack before filling.

If recipe specifies an unbaked shell, don't prick pastry. Spoon in filling. Bake as directed in recipe. Makes one 9-inch shell.

1 1/2 cups Ranch House Baking mix
3 tbsp Vegetable shortening
1 tsp active dry yeast
1/2 tsp sugar
3 tbsp warm water
1 tsp evaporated milk

Place baking mix into medium bowl. Cut in shortening with a pastry blender until coarse particles form; set aside.

Stir together yeast, sugar and warm water in a 1-cup measure; let stand until bubbly, 5 to 10 minutes. Add to baking mix, along with the evaporated milk. Stir with a spoon until dough leaves the sides of bowl. Continue stirring 2 minutes until smooth and pliable. Dough should be just soft enough to shape without crumbling if pressing into place, or crumbling or sticking if rolling out on a floured surface. If too dry add a small amount of cold water. If too soft add a small amount of baking mix.

Shape, fill and bake as directed in individual recipes. The pastry may be used for main dish pastry shells, turn-overs, appetizers and casserole toppings.

WAFFLES

For a quick satisfying meal serve waffles with sausage, bacon or ham. Waffles have been long removed from the breakfast-only category. When planning brunch or supper menus, add them to your list. Creamed foods, such as Chicken a la King or Creamed Chipped Beef served over hot waffles creates a pleasant change from toast. Chocolate Waffles takes the place of cake when served with ice cream, topped with hot fudge sauce. Or serve sweetened crushed strawberries over a warm waffle, topped with whipped cream for dessert. When a brisk winter wind is blowing, serve spicy Ginger Waffles with warm Rum Molasses Syrup for a day brightner.

The consistency of waffle batter is thicker than batter made for pancakes. More butter or shortening is used in waffle batter, making greasing unnecessary after a new iron has been seasoned. When ready to bake waffles, follow the manufacturers instructions, and select temperature indicated for lightly browned or well browned waffles as desired. Waffle batter spreads as it heats. Pour in just enough batter in center of each compartment to fill grid as it heats without overflowing. (Irons vary in size. Learn the amount of batter needed to bake a waffle that fills the iron evenly.) Do not raise cover until waffle puffs and stops steaming, about 5 minutes. If it is raised too soon, the waffle splits crosswise. If this occurs, immediately lower cover and continue baking a few minutes longer until lightly browned. When waffle is done loosen edges with a fork, remove to warm plate. Serve immediately.

Store leftover waffles in refrigerator 3 or 4 days, or wrap well in plastic wrap and freeze 3 months. To reheat waffles, thaw first if frozen. Place on a baking sheet. Heat in oven 325°, uncovered, 5 minutes. Turn, continue heating about 5 minutes or until hot.

BASIC WAFFLES

1 2/3 cups Ranch House Baking Mix
1 cup milk
1 egg, beaten
2 tsp sugar
3 tbsp melted butter or margarine, cooled

Place baking mix, milk, egg and sugar
into a 4-cup measure with a pouring
spout. Stir with beaters to dampen,
beat at medium speed 15 seconds. Scrape
container with a rubber spatula. Stir
in melted butter. Pour batter into a
square 4 compartment 9-inch hot waffle
iron. Close and bake until lightly browned.
makes six 4 1/2-inch waffles.

CHOCOLATE WAFFLES

1 3/4 cups Ranch House Baking Mix
1/3 cup sugar
1/4 cup cocoa powder
1/8 tsp baking soda
3/4 cup milk
2 eggs, beaten
3 Tbsp melted butter, cooled

Place baking mix, sugar, cocoa and baking soda into a 4-cup measure with a pouring spout. Stir with a pastry blender until well mixed. Add milk and eggs. Stir with beaters to dampen, beat at medium speed 15 seconds. Scrape container with a rubber spatula. Stir in melted butter. Pour batter into a square 4 compartment 9-inch hot waffle iron. Close and bake until lightly browned. Makes 7 cake-type 4 1/2-inch waffles.

NOTE: If waffles stick to waffle iron, loosen edges with a fork for easy removal.

CHOCOLATE PECAN WAFFLES

1 3/4 cups Ranch House Baking mix
1/3 cup sweetened chocolate beverage powder
1/4 tsp cinnamon
1/8 tsp baking soda
3/4 cup milk
2 eggs, beaten
6 tbsp medium to finely chopped pecans
3 tbsp melted butter, cooled

Place baking mix, chocolate powder, cinnamon and baking soda into a 4-cup measure with a pouring spout. Stir with a pastry blender until well mixed. Add milk and eggs. Stir with beaters to dampen, beat at medium speed 15 seconds. Scrape container with a rubber spatula. Stir in chopped pecans and melted butter. Pour batter into a square 4 compartment 9-inch hot waffle iron. Close and bake until lightly browned. Gently stir batter before pouring each batch of waffles. Makes seven 4 1/2-inch waffles.

NOTE: If waffles stick to waffle iron, loosen edges with a fork for easy removal.

CORNMEAL WAFFLES

2 eggs
3/4 cup buttermilk
1/2 cup evaporated milk
1 1/2 cups Ranch House Baking Mix
3/4 cup yellow stone ground cornmeal
2 tsp sugar
1/4 tsp each baking soda and baking powder
1/8 tsp salt
3 tbsp lukewarm bacon drippings

Beat eggs in a 4-cup measure with a pouring spout. Blend in buttermilk and evaporated milk. Combine baking mix, cornmeal, sugar, baking soda, baking powder and salt in medium bowl. Blend well with a pastry blender. Add to egg mixture. Stir with beaters to dampen, beat at medium speed 15 seconds. Scrape container with a rubber spatula. Stir in bacon drippings. If batter needs thinning, add a small amount of evaporated milk. Pour batter into a square 4 compartment 9-inch hot waffle iron. Close and bake until golden brown. Makes eight 4 1/2-inch waffles.

DELUXE BUTTERMILK WAFFLES

1 1/2 cups Ranch House Baking mix
1 tbsp sugar
1/8 tsp baking soda
3/4 cup buttermilk
2 eggs, beaten
3 tbsp melted butter, cooled

Place baking mix, sugar and baking soda into a 4-cup measure with a pouring spout. Stir with a fork to blend. Add buttermilk and eggs. Stir with beaters to dampen, beat at medium speed 15 seconds. Scrape container with a rubber spatula. Stir in melted butter. Pour batter into a square 4 compartment 9-inch hot waffle iron. Close and bake until lightly browned. makes six 4 1/2-inch waffles.

GINGER WAFFLES

2 cups Ranch House Baking Mix
1 tsp each ginger and cinnamon
1/4 tsp each nutmeg and allspice
1/8 tsp baking soda
3/4 cup milk
6 tbsp light molasses
2 eggs, beaten
1/4 cup melted butter, cooled

Place baking mix, spices and baking soda into a 4-cup measure with a pouring spout. Stir with a fork to blend. Add milk, molasses and eggs. Stir with beaters to dampen, beat at medium speed 15 seconds. Scrape container with a rubber spatula. Stir in melted butter. Pour batter into a square 4 compartment 9-inch hot waffle iron. Close and bake until golden brown. Makes seven 4 1/2-inch waffles. Serve with warm Rum Molasses Syrup. (P-558)

NOTE: If waffles stick to waffle iron, loosen edges with a fork for easy removal.

PUMPKIN WAFFLES

2 eggs
1 cup Pumpkin Pie mix, from a 21-oz can
1/4 cup cooking oil
1/4 cup light molasses
2 cups Ranch House Baking mix
1/2 cup evaporated milk

Beat eggs in a 4-cup measure with a pouring spout. Blend in pie mix, oil and molasses. Add baking mix and evaporated milk. Stir with beaters to dampen, beat at medium speed 15 seconds. Scrape container with a rubber spatula. (Batter will be thick.) Pour into a square 4 compartment 9-inch waffle iron. Close and bake until golden brown. Waffles will be soft and cake-like. Serve with warm Rum molasses syrup. (P-558) makes eight 4½-inch waffles.

SOUTHERN WAFFLES

2 egg yolks
1 cup buttermilk
1/2 cup light cream
2 1/4 cups Ranch House Baking Mix
1/8 tsp baking soda
1/4 cup melted butter, cooled
2 egg whites
1 1/2 tbsp sugar

Beat egg yolks in a 4-cup measure with a pouring spout. Blend in buttermilk and cream. Combine baking mix and soda. Add to buttermilk mixture. Stir with beaters to dampen, beat at medium speed 15 seconds. Scrape container with a rubber spatula. Stir in melted butter; set aside.

Beat egg whites in medium bowl until foamy. Add sugar, beat until soft peaks form. Fold in 1/4 of the batter, then gradually fold egg white mixture into remaining batter. Pour batter into a square 4 compartment 9-inch hot waffle iron. Close and bake until lightly browned. Makes eight 4 1/2-inch waffles.

INDEX
Part 2

CHICKEN (ASSORTED)
Chicken Pie, 463
Chicken Stew and Dumplings, 465
Mexicali Chicken Casserole, 466
Royal Chicken Casserole, 468
Smothered Chicken, 470
"Souper" Baked Chicken, 471
Swiss Chicken Casserole, 472

PIES (ENTRÉE)
Beef Stroganoff Pie, 474
Chicken Pie (P. 463, Assorted Chicken)
Ham and Cheese Pie, 476
Knockwurst Pie, 477
Swiss Soufflé Pie, 479
Yorkshire Beef Pie, 480

PUFFS (ENTRÉE)
Entrée Puff Shells, 482
Beef Stroganoff Puffs, 484
Chicken Puffs, 485
Hot Dog Puffs, 486
Shrimp Puffs, 487
Swiss Cheese and Ham Puffs, 488

QUICHE (CRUSTLESS)
Crustless Bacon and Corn Quiche, 489
Crustless Beef and Cheddar Quiche, 490
Crustless Green Chilies Quiche, 491
Crustless Ham Quiche, 492
Crustless Mexican Quiche, 493
Crustless Shrimp Quiche, 494
Crustless Turkey Quiche, 495

SANDWICHES
Bacon and Cheese Buns, 496
Barbecue Beef Buns, 497
BLT and Guacamole Buns, 498
Chicken Salad Buns, 499
Corn Beef Buns, 500

Bonus

MORE DELICIOUS RECIPES

To Enjoy

SPANISH BEEF STEW AND DUMPLINGS

2 lbs beef for stew, cut into 1 to 1 1/2-inch cubes
2 cups hot water
1 16-oz can tomatoes
1 8-oz can tomato sauce
1 6-oz can tomato paste
1 large onion, peeled and diced
3/4 cup frozen diced green peppers
1 1/2 tbsp chili powder
1 1/2 tsp seasoned salt
1/2 tsp each paprika, garlic powder, ground
 cumin, ground coriander and oregano leaves
1 bay leaf

DUMPLINGS
1 1/2 cups Ranch House Baking mix
1/2 cup milk

Place stew ingredients into Dutch oven. Stir until blended. Bring to boiling over high heat. Cover. Transfer stew to oven preheated at 300°. Bake until almost tender, about 3 to 3 1/2. Transfer to stove top. Dip a tablespoon into the simmering stew then into dumpling dough. Scoop up heaping spoonfuls, drop on top of stew in 4 equal portions. Cook over low heat, uncovered, 8 minutes. Cover, cook 8 minutes longer. makes 4 servings.

DUMPLINGS: Place baking mix into small bowl. Add milk, stir quickly with a fork until a soft drop dough forms; let stand 5 minutes.

CHEESY HOT DOG BUNS

6 hot dogs, cut into 1/4-inch cubes
6-oz Cheddar cheese, cut into 1/4-inch cubes
2 green onions, finely chopped
1 tbsp chopped chilies, deseeded
1/4 cup mayonnaise
1/4 cup bottled chili sauce or catsup
2 Tsp hot dog relish
4 SANDWICH BUNS for steaks (recipe in yeast bread section p-)

Place hot dogs, cheese, green onions and chilies in medium bowl. Combine mayonnaise, chili sauce or catsup and hot dog relish in a 1-cup measure. Stir into hot dog mixture until well blended. Cut buns in half lengthwise. Spread filling over bottom half, dividing evenly. Top with upper half of bun. Wrap in foil. Place package on a baking sheet.

Heat in oven 350° 22 minutes. makes 4 servings.

BARBECUE ROAST PORK WITH DUMPLINGS

4 lb Boston Butt or Picnic shoulder pork roast
1 15-oz can solid pack tomatoes
1/2 cup cider Vinegar
1/3 cup brown sugar, pkd
1/4 cup worcestershire sauce
2 tsp seasoned salt
1 1/2 tsp crushed red pepper
1/2 tsp black pepper
1/4 tsp barbecue spice

DUMPLINGS
2 cups Ranch House Baking mix
3/4 tsp barbecue spice
1/2 cup plus 1 tbsp milk

Trim excess fat from pork, then place roast
in Dutch oven. Adjust oven rack to lower level,
then preheat to 400°. Roast meat, uncovered 45 minutes.

Place tomatoes, Vinegar, brown sugar, worcestershire
sauce and seasonings into electric blender container.
Blend at low speed until smooth. Spoon off fat
in Dutch oven. Pour tomato mixture over pork; stir
well. Cover pot. Lower oven temperature to 325°.
Roast meat until tender, about 3 hours. Remove
to platter. Place sauce in bowl. Cool meat and
sauce, then chill 4 hours. Remove congealed fat
from sauce, then place sauce in large saucepan.
Heat over low-to-medium heat until hot. Slice
meat to desired thickness, then place in sauce.

Cover saucepan. Simmer 15 minutes over low heat. Serve with dumplings and rice or noodles. Makes 6 servings.

DUMPLINGS: Place 2 quarts hot water into dutch oven. Bring to boiling while preparing dumplings. Place baking mix and barbecue spice into medium bowl. Add milk, stir quickly with a fork until barely mixed. If dough seems stiff add a small amount of milk, about 1/2 to 1 tablespoon, stir quickly until a soft dough forms; let stand 5 minutes. With a rubber spatula remove dough to a floured surface. With floured hands round up into a ball. Lightly coat with flour, knead lightly 8 times. Pat out with floured hand into a rectangle 6 by 4-inches. Cut dough lengthwise in half, then cut crosswise in thirds. Drop into boiling water. Immediately lower heat until water is gently simmering. Cook, uncovered, 7 minutes. Cover, cook 6 minutes longer. Makes 6 dumplings.

HUNGARIAN BEEF PIE

1 tbsp each butter and vegetable shortening
1 1/2 lbs beef for stew, cut into 3/4 to 1-inch cubes
1 cup frozen chopped onions, unthawed
1 8-oz can tomato sauce
1/2 tbsp each worcestershire sauce and brown sugar
1 tsp each paprika and dill weed
1/2 tsp each garlic salt, seasoned salt and
    basil leaves
1/4 tsp pepper
3 cups hot water
1 1/2 cups 1/2 to 3/4-inch peeled potato cubes
1/2 cup sour cream
PRESS-IN PASTRY TOPPING; recipe follows

Fry meat in butter and shortening in Dutch
oven over medium-to-high heat until well
browned on all sides. Push meat to one side
of pot. Add onions. Sauté over medium
heat 10 minutes, stirring occasionally. Stir
onions into meat. Add tomato sauce, worcestershire, brown sugar, paprika, dill, garlic
salt, seasoned salt, basil and pepper. Stir
until well blended. Stir in hot water.
Bring to boiling, then turn heat off. Cover
pot. Transfer to oven preheated to 300°.
Bake until meat is almost tender, about
3 hours. Transfer to stove top. Add
potato cubes. Cover. Simmer until potatoes
are tender and gravy is thick, about 15 to
18 minutes. Gently blend sour cream into
gravy with a large slotted spoon. Cook

over low heat until gravy is hot, but do not boil. Spoon into four 12-oz pottery or glass casseroles. Top with hot pastry. Makes 4 servings.

PRESS-IN PASTRY TOPPING: Place 1 cup plus 2 tablespoons Ranch House Baking mix into small bowl. Cut in 2 1/2 tablespoons Vegetable shortening with a pastry blender until coarse particles form. Gradually sprinkle about 1 1/2 tablespoon cold water over mixture, blending together with a fork. Add just enough water to form a pliable dough. Round up into a smooth ball. Divide into 4 equal pieces. Roll into smooth balls between palms of hands. Place balls on on ungreased baking sheet about 4 1/2-inches apart. Press into 4 1/2-inch rounds.

Bake at 400° 6 to 8 minutes or until a light golden color. Do not overbake. Cool 5 minutes. Lift pastry onto top of casseroles just before serving.

NOTE: The pastry may be baked ahead, then reheated on a baking sheet in 325° oven 5 to 7 minutes, just before serving.

TUNA SKILLET CASSEROLE

1 10 3/4-oz can cream of chicken soup
1 cup milk
1/2 tsp onion powder
1/4 tsp Lemon 'N Herb seasoning
1/8 tsp pepper
1 13-oz can chunk tuna, drained and
  coarsely flaked
3 hard-cooked eggs, cut in half

CORNBREAD TOPPING
1 egg
1 tbsp cooking oil
2/3 cup buttermilk
1 cup Ranch House Baking Mix
1/2 cup yellow stone ground cornmeal
3/4 tsp sugar
1/8 tsp each baking soda and salt

Spoon soup into 8 1/2 to 9-inch heavy
iron skillet. Gradually stir in milk. Add
seasonings. Cook and stir over medium heat
until mixture starts to bubble. Stir in
tuna. Turn heat off. Add eggs, cut side up,
pushing tuna mixture aside to cover eggs.

Bake at 400° 20 minutes. Remove
from oven. Place a large baking sheet in
oven to catch spills. Pour topping over
tuna; starting at outer edge, make a complete
circle. Continue pouring batter in circles until
tuna is completely covered. Gently spread
batter to make an even layer. Return

to oven, placing skillet in center of baking sheet. Continue baking at 400° 20 minutes until topping is lightly browned. Cool 10 minutes. Makes 3 servings.

CORNBREAD TOPPING: Beat egg in small bowl. Blend in buttermilk and oil at low speed. Combine baking mix, cornmeal, sugar, baking soda and salt in small bowl with a pastry blender. Add to buttermilk mixture. Stir with beaters to dampen, beat at low speed 1/2 minute. Scrape bowl with a rubber spatula, stir 10 turns.

CHILI RELLENOS CASSEROLE

3 4-oz cans whole green chilies
2 cups (8-oz) grated Jack cheese
2 eggs
1 cup milk
3/4 cup Ranch House Baking mix
1/8 tsp salt
3/4 cup hot enchilada sauce from a 10-oz can
3/4 cup tomato juice

Drain chilies; remove seeds. Coat an 8-inch square glass baking dish with non-stick vegetable spray. Place 1/2 of the chilies in the bottom of dish, making an even layer. Sprinkle with 1 1/2 cups of the grated cheese. Layer remaining chilies over the cheese; set aside.

Place eggs, milk, baking mix and salt into electric blender container. Blend at medium speed 1 minute. Scrape down sides of container with a rubber spatula. Blend at medium speed 1/2 minute. Pour mixture over chilies. Sprinkle with remaining grated cheese.

Bake at 350° 22 minutes. (While casserole is baking, combine enchilada sauce and tomato juice in small saucepan. Bring to a simmer over medium heat). Spoon 1/2 cup of the enchilada sauce mixture over top of casserole. Bake 15 minutes longer. Cool 10 minutes. Serve with the remaining sauce on the side. Makes 4 servings.

MEXICAN CASSEROLE

FILLING

1 1/4 lbs lean ground beef
1 cup chopped onion
1/2 cup chopped green pepper
1/4 cup hot water
1 1/4 cups commercial Italian sauce
2 tbsp chili powder
3/4 tsp seasoned salt
1/4 tsp garlic salt

TOPPING

2 eggs
3/4 cup milk
1 cup Ranch House Baking mix
1/4 cup cornmeal
1/8 tsp salt
1 1/2 cups (6-oz) grated jalapeno jack cheese

FILLING: Fry ground beef in Dutch oven over medium-to-high heat until red color leaves meat. Spoon off all but 1 tablespoon fat. Push meat to one side of pot. Add onion and green pepper. Fry over low heat until almost tender, stirring occasionally. Combine with meat. Continue cooking until meat is lightly browned. Stir in hot water. Add

Italian sauce, chili powder, seasoned salt and garlic salt. Bring to boiling over high heat, then lower heat until mixture is simmering. Cook, uncovered, 5 minutes. Spoon into a lightly greased 10-inch square baking pan, spreading to make an even layer. Spoon with topping.

Bake at 375° 20 minutes. Sprinkle 3/4 cup grated cheese over topping. Bake 10 minutes longer. Cool 10 minutes. Makes 6 servings.

TOPPING: Beat eggs in medium bowl. Add milk, baking mix, cornmeal and salt. Stir with beaters to dampen, beat at low speed 20 seconds. Stir in 3/4 cup of the grated cheese.

CRUSTLESS TURKEY DIVAN QUICHE

saute if recipe is good

1 10-oz pkg frozen broccoli spears
1/4 cup mayonnaise, 2 tbsp milk
1 egg yolk
2 tbsp grated Parmesan cheese
1 tsp lemon juice
1/8 tsp dry mustard
1/16 tsp pepper
1 cup coarsely chopped leftover roast turkey,
   lightly pkd in cup
3 eggs
1 1/2 cups milk
1/2 cups Ranch House Baking Mix
1/4 tsp salt
1/8 tsp pepper
1 cup (4-oz) grated Cheddar cheese

Cook broccoli as directed on package. Cool until lukewarm. Drain well. Cut into 1-inch chunks. Grease a 10-inch glass pie pan. Layer broccoli into bottom of pan. Combine milk, mayonnaise, egg yolk, grated cheese, lemon juice, mustard and pepper in small bowl. Blend at low speed 1/2 minute. Spoon over broccoli. Sprinkle chopped turkey over broccoli layer. Press with fingers to make an even layer.

MEDIUM WHITE SAUCE

1/4 cup butter or margarine
1/4 cup flour
2 1/2 cups milk
salt and pepper to taste

Melt butter or margarine in 8 1/2-inch skillet over low heat. Stir in flour with a fork. Remove skillet from heat; gradually stir in 1 cup of the milk. Return to medium heat; gradually stir in remaining milk. Cook and stir until sauce thickens. Add salt and pepper to taste. Makes about 2 1/2 cups sauce.

EASY CHICKEN OR BEEF GRAVY

R

1 cup hot water
2 tsp instant chicken or beef bouillon granules
1/4 tsp onion powder
pepper to taste
1/3 cup milk
2 1/2 tbsp instant flour
(a drop or 2 of yellow food color, and a dash of
poultry seasoning for the chicken gravy)
1 tbsp butter

Combine hot water, bouillon and seasoning in small saucepan. Bring to boiling over medium heat. Combine milk and flour in a 1-cup measure. Stir into broth. Cook and stir over low heat until smooth and thickened. Stir in butter until melted. If gravy needs thinning, add a small amount of milk until desired consistency is reached. (For chicken gravy, stir in food color and poultry seasoning last.) makes 1 1/4 cups gravy (about)

O.K.

QUICK BEEF GRAVY

2 tbsp butter or margarine
2 tbsp flour
1 cup hot water
1/2 tsp onion powder
1 tsp instant beef bouillon granules
1 tbsp hot water

Melt butter in small saucepan (if making double measure, use small skillet.) Stir in flour with a fork. Remove from heat. Gradually stir in hot water. Add onion powder. Return to medium heat. Cook and stir until mixture thickens. Combine beef bouillon and 1 tablespoon hot water. Add to gravy. Cook and stir until smooth. Makes about 1 cup gravy.

O.K.

QUICK CHICKEN GRAVY

1 cup hot water
1 tbsp butter or margarine
1 tsp instant chicken bouillon granules
1/4 tsp onion powder
a sprinkle of poultry seasoning; optional
1/4 cup milk
2 1/2 tbsp instant flour
pepper to taste

Place hot water, butter, bouillon, onion powder and poultry seasoning into small saucepan. Bring to boiling over medium heat. Combine milk and instant flour in a 1-cup measure. Stir into simmering liquid. Cook and stir until smooth and thick. Add pepper to taste. Makes about 1 1/4 cups gravy.

NOTE these gravies may be used as a base for making topping and fillings for YORKSHIRE PANCAKES, ENTREE PUFFS and hot sandwiches. Add cooked sausage, diced ham, shrimp, etc, to gravy base.

Chicken & Gravy Notes

→ 1 3 to 3 1/2 lb broiler-fryer, cut up

  or

→ 1 broiler-fryer (about 3 1/2 pounds) cut up ~~yields a minimum of 2 1/2 cups cooked chicken chunks~~

→ If making a baked casserole dish, allow 1 cup medium consistency gravy for each 1 cups 1-inch chicken chunks.

→ For medium consistency gravy use:
  1/4 cup butter
  1/4 cup flour
  2 1/4 cups milk

→ 1 3 to 3 1/2 lb broiler-fryer, cut up, placed in Dutch oven with 2 cups water yields 2 3/4 to 3 cups broth.

  → If using 1 1/2 cups water, broth yield will be around 2 cups broth

  → It takes about 45 to 50 minutes to cook chicken until tender.

ALL PURPOSE CHEESE SAUCE

3 Tbsp butter or margarine
1/4 cup flour
2 1/4 cups milk
1 tsp Worcestershire sauce
1/2 tsp onion powder
1 cup (4-oz) grated sharp Cheddar cheese
salt and pepper to taste

Melt butter or margarine in 8 1/2-inch skillet over low heat. Stir in flour with a fork. Remove skillet from heat; gradually stir in 1 cup of the milk. Return to medium heat; gradually stir in remaining milk. Cook and stir until sauce thickens. Add Worcestershire sauce, onion powder and grated cheese. Cook and stir until cheese melts and sauce is smooth. Add salt and pepper to taste. Serve over baked potatoes, toast, biscuits, macaroni, etc. Makes about 2 3/4 cups sauce.

ITALIAN MAC-BEEF CASSEROLE

CRUST
1 1/4 cups Ranch House Baking Mix
2 tbsp vegetable shortening
2 tbsp plus 1 tsp cold water

BEEF FILLING
1 lb lean ground beef
1 1/2 cups commercial or homemade italian sauce
1/2 tsp each seasoned salt and onion powder
1/4 tsp each garlic powder, pepper, ground coriander,
   basil and oregano leaves, crumbled

TOPPING
1/4 cup butter or margarine
1/4 cup flour
1 3/4 cups milk
1/2 tsp onion powder
1/4 tsp salt
1/8 tsp pepper
2 cups cooked elbow macaroni
1/2 cup grated Mozzarella cheese (4-oz)
1/2 cup grated Jack cheese (4-oz)
1/4 cup grated Parmesan cheese from a can

CRUST: Place baking mix into small
bowl. Cut in shortening with a pastry blender
until coarse particles form. Gradually sprinkle
cold water over mixture, blending together with
a fork; add just enough water to form a pliable
dough. Round up into a smooth ball. Place
tablespoons of dough at close intervals on
bottom of a 9-inch square baking pan.
Press with fingers to evenly cover bottom

and 1/2-inch up sides of pan; set aside.

BEEF FILLING: Fry ground beef in Dutch oven over medium-to-high heat until red color leaves meat, breaking up chunks as it cooks. Spoon off fat. Add remaining ingredients. Cook over low-to-medium heat until mixture thickens, about 15 minutes, stirring occasionally. Remove from heat. Cool.

TOPPING: Melt butter in medium skillet over low heat. Stir in flour until well blended. Remove from heat. Gradually stir in 1 cup of the milk. Return to low-to-medium heat. Gradually stir in remaining milk. Cook and stir until mixture thickens. Stir in seasonings, then stir in cooked macaroni. Turn heat off.

Spread beef filling evenly over crust. Spoon with macaroni topping. In small bowl combine grated mozzarella, Jack and Parmesan cheese. Sprinkle evenly over macaroni topping.

Bake at 375° 25 to 30 minutes until lightly browned on top. Cool 15 minutes before serving. Makes 4 servings.

NOTE: To make 8 servings double crust, filling and topping ingredients. Assemble in 14 by 10-inch baking pan. Bake at 375° 30 to 35 minutes. This casserole makes a great patio party entree, served with a tossed salad and hot garlic bread. Leftover casserole reheats nicely. Cut into serving. Place in a small baking pan. Cover top of pan with well vented foil. Heat at 325° 22 minutes.

This is a book of inspiration that is worth sharing

Available for downloading at: https://besteasyrecipes.blog/

Available in two volumes at Amazon.com

www.ingramcontent.com/pod-product-compliance
Lightning Source LLC
Chambersburg PA
CBHW050744100426
42739CB00016BA/3437